Cambridge Elements

Elements in Environmental Humanities
edited by
Louise Westling
University of Oregon
Serenella Iovino
University of North Carolina at Chapel Hill
Timo Maran
University of Tartu

RUIN ECOLOGY

An Exercise in Environmental Imagination

Marco Malvestio
University of Padua

Shaftesbury Road, Cambridge CB2 8EA, United Kingdom

One Liberty Plaza, 20th Floor, New York, NY 10006, USA

477 Williamstown Road, Port Melbourne, VIC 3207, Australia

314–321, 3rd Floor, Plot 3, Splendor Forum, Jasola District Centre,
New Delhi – 110025, India

103 Penang Road, #05–06/07, Visioncrest Commercial, Singapore 238467

Cambridge University Press is part of Cambridge University Press & Assessment, a department of the University of Cambridge.

We share the University's mission to contribute to society through the pursuit of education, learning and research at the highest international levels of excellence.

www.cambridge.org
Information on this title: www.cambridge.org/9781009683029
DOI: 10.1017/9781009683036

© Marco Malvestio 2025

This publication is in copyright. Subject to statutory exception and to the provisions of relevant collective licensing agreements, no reproduction of any part may take place without the written permission of Cambridge University Press & Assessment.

When citing this work, please include a reference to the DOI 10.1017/9781009683036

First published 2025

A catalogue record for this publication is available from the British Library

ISBN 978-1-009-68302-9 Hardback
ISBN 978-1-009-68301-2 Paperback
ISSN 2632-3125 (online)
ISSN 2632-3117 (print)

Cambridge University Press & Assessment has no responsibility for the persistence or accuracy of URLs for external or third-party internet websites referred to in this publication and does not guarantee that any content on such websites is, or will remain, accurate or appropriate.

For EU product safety concerns, contact us at Calle de José Abascal, 56, 1°, 28003 Madrid, Spain, or email eugpsr@cambridge.org

Ruin Ecology

An Exercise in Environmental Imagination

Elements in Environmental Humanities

DOI: 10.1017/9781009683036
First published online: October 2025

Marco Malvestio
University of Padua

Author for correspondence: Marco Malvestio, marco.malvestio@unipd.it

Abstract: This Element discusses the presence of ruins in contemporary environmental imagination. Contemporary ruins, much more than those that served as constituents of Romantic and Gothic aesthetics, simultaneously express a fascination with and a dread of the non-human agencies at play in the world while also countering the nostalgic dimension of traditional representations of ruins. The contemporary success of ruins can be connected to the sense of planetary precarity induced by anthropogenic climate change, and to the widespread presence of eco-anxiety in the public conscience. Moreover, at the centre of ruins' aesthetic power is the interaction of human and non-human forces, and in the process of ruination, buildings and monuments find new meaning, thanks to the intervention of external agents that human civilization has long attempted to tame or eliminate and that make a disturbing return as soon as anthropic activity ceases.

Keywords: ruins, environmental humanities, ecocriticism, comparative literature, Gothic

© Marco Malvestio 2025

ISBNs: 9781009683029 (HB), 9781009683012 (PB), 9781009683036 (OC)
ISSNs: 2632-3125 (online), 2632-3117 (print)

Contents

Introduction: Dreaming among Ruins	1
1 A New *Ruinenlust*	7
2 The World without Whom?	22
3 An Ecology of Negativity	35
4 The Promises of Ghosts	49
Conclusion: The State of Things to Come	62
References	64

Ruin Ecology 1

> Seasons turn
> Ruins alive
> Bridges burn
> All things will drown
> Ash and debris
> The state of things to come
> — Shores of Null, *Ruins Alive*

Introduction: Dreaming among Ruins

An essential constituent of the imagination of modernity, ruins have, over the last two centuries, been extensively represented and theorized as manifestations of the effects of time, the greater power of nature over human agency, and the impermanence of human activities. As cultural artefacts, in the eighteenth and nineteenth centuries ruins provided the backbone for political thought and for aesthetic theories, most importantly that of the sublime. Yet, ruins are not a matter of the past, but of the present, and their representation plays a pivotal role in environmental imagination. We live in an age of renewed *Ruinenlust*, or, to employ a controversial term that encapsulates the ubiquity of ruins in present-day media, of ruin porn: we find ruins in science fiction movies and social media accounts devoted to urban exploration, in political discourse and tourism; most importantly, we find them in conceptualizations of the current climate and environmental crisis, and in discussions of environmental justice.

When compared to the *Ruinenlust* of old, however, a crucial difference should immediately be noticed: the ruins we represent, ruins that populate our fantasies and are scattered across our cities, are not those of a distant past, but those of our present. In contemporary imagery, ruins stand out less, in comparison with the monuments immortalized in traditional ruin painting and engraving, but are also more pervasive – as both physical and cultural artefacts. This Element does not discuss ruins as exceptional spaces, but rather as everyday ones: even when describing unique places like Fukushima, or science-fictional landscapes, the ruins evoked in these pages prove to be quite familiar, certainly more so than the decrepit Roman arenas and medieval abbeys so often portrayed in the eighteenth and nineteenth centuries.

In this Element, I argue that contemporary ruins, much more than those that served as the backbone of Romantic and Gothic aesthetics, simultaneously express a fascination with and a dread of the non-human agencies at play in the world. Ruins tend to represent these feelings in terms coherent with recent theorizations of the Anthropocene sublime, and force us to recover the conceptual and aesthetic framework of the Gothic to discuss the endangered environments of present-day Earth. Specifically, the central hypotheses of this Element are that, in contemporary imagination, ruins force us to confront an increasingly dangerous planet, the generic instability and perishability of things associated with ruins being substituted with more specific human-made disasters; that they force us to face the capillary presence of non-human agencies in our lives and everyday spaces, a presence that our culture tends to consistently disregard; and, finally, that they unsettle and contest human chronologies in ways that are simultaneously productive and confusing for our understanding of what being in the world means.

In other words, this Element participates in a tendency, developed in recent years across the environmental humanities, towards what I would call a 'negative ecology':[1] a kind of ecological discourse and practice that involves taking into account what is culturally and socially considered marginal, derelict, invisible. If early ecocritical enquiries were largely focused on the pastoral mode (of which ruins are often a scenic constituent), contemporary ideas in the environmental humanities, from Donna Haraway's Chthulhucene (2016) to Timothy Morton's 'dark ecology' (2018) to the many theorizations of waste, have shown how fruitful it can be to look not at the 'official' representations of the natural world – the pastoral and idealized – but rather at their margins, where nature and culture most productively intersect. In this sense, discussing ruins means contributing to the wider discourse about waste, but also about non-human agencies found in unlikely places, where our culture would not normally place them, from fungi and slime (Estok 2025) to compost (Hamilton and Neimanis 2018; Ferrante 2022) to the mineral world (Cohen 2015; Luisetti 2023). A negative ecology is one that takes into account the discarded, what we usually see as useless and dangerous, and that from the margins contests the very notion of balance and hierarchy in the world, showing the precarity of human life on a planet that teems with other agencies – where agency is viewed as 'a pervasive and inbuilt property of matter, as part and parcel of its generative dynamism' (Iovino and Opperman 2014, 3).

Ruins, as we have already mentioned, are a Gothic topic and trope, and have characterized Gothic imagination since its inception. The ruined palace wings of Udolpho, the crumbling walls of the Usher mansion, the vast array of decrepit crypts and abandoned churches we find in novels, paintings, illustrations, and movies, are the essential setting for the return of the repressed characteristic of Gothic imagination. While only Section 3 is explicitly devoted to modern iterations of this genre, Gothic theory and imagery permeate and inform this whole Element at some level: in order to describe a negative ecology, in other words, it is essential to mobilize a negative aesthetics. A negative ecology is

---

[1] I borrow the term from McGrath (2019), who, however, employs it in a different manner.

also, inevitably, an ecogothic one, meaning one that highlights 'the fear, anxiety, and dread' regulating the relationships between human and non-human worlds (Keetley and Sivils 2017, 1), and such a framework proves to be especially helpful in addressing the peculiar ambiguity in relation to non-human agencies associated with contemporary ruins.

It is not by chance that I have used the word 'framework'. A common trope in ruin painting (one could even say an architectural *Pathosformel*), particularly with medieval subjects, is the depiction of the windows of ruined buildings as the central or main part of the composition. Caspar David Friedrich's *Ruins of the Oybin Monastery (The Dreamer)* (ca. 1835; see Figure 1) is an especially famous iteration of this trope, but many other examples could be mobilized – even among contemporary artists, as we will see. This recurring type of

Figure 1 Caspar David Friedrich, *Ruins of the Oybin Monastery (The Dreamer)*, ca. 1835. Public domain (Wikicommons).

composition features the windows of ruined buildings, beyond whose glassless openings one can see scenery, either containing other ruins or, more frequently, natural elements. In Friedrich, the windows of the ruined monastery quite literally transform into a liminal space, and become a point of passage between the human, yet abandoned, realm of the building and the indefinite, evocative natural landscape beyond. The term used to describe the human figure in the title, the dreamer, is indicative of this function of passage and transition associated with ruins, as if the mind of the character had already embarked on an oneiric journey. Yet, something else happens in this picture: the ruined building *frames* the landscape beyond, with its trees and sunset, and forces viewers to re-contextualize it and to ponder the meaning and function of these natural elements in relation to ruins. In this sense, we shall see how thinking about ruins (using ruins as a framework to understand the present) means re-thinking the natural world that lays beyond, and in, them, and, most importantly, our relationship with it. Like the figure in the painting, we too must become dreamers at the threshold and accept the ruin as 'revelation, a rhetoric of things to come' (Wood 2021, xii).

As can be easily imagined, this is not, and cannot be, an Element about ruins in general. Such a scope would vastly exceed the limits of this Element, as ruins have almost continuously been at the core of philosophical and aesthetic reflections for the last three centuries. From classics like Walter Benjamin's *Origin of the German Trauerspiel* (2019) to Rose Macaulay's *Pleasure of Ruins* (1953) to Paul Zucker's *Fascination of Decay* (1968) to Francesco Orlando's *Obsolete Objects in the Literary Imagination: Ruins, Relics, Rarities, Rubbish, Uninhabited places, and Hidden Treasures* (2006), the topic of ruins has elicited the interest of critics all around the globe and from all disciplines. Similarly, in the last thirty years, museums and art institutions have provided several explorations of the topic across visual arts, as in the case of exhibitions like *Irresistible Decay: Ruins Reclaimed* (Research Library of the Getty Research Institute, 1997), *Visions of Ruin* (Sir John Soane's Museum, 1999), *The Ruins of Detroit* (Wilmotte Gallery at Lichfield Studios in London, 2012), and *Ruin Lust*, curated by Brian Dillon at Tate Britain (2014) (Apel 2015, 9).[2]

As much as ruins have been discussed in contemporary scholarship, however, they seem to be addressed mostly in the fields of anthropology, philosophy, cultural geography, and architecture. Discussions of ruins from an environmental perspective are rarer, and most of those that do exist are devoted to physical ruins (and the opportunities they pose for processes of rewilding) rather than

---

[2] Besides the sources directly quoted in the article, see Jackson 1980; Augé 2003; Huyssen 2010; Hatherley 2010; Porter 2011; Pétursdóttir and Olsen 2014b; Harbison 2015; Orvell 2021.

their representations. This Element, on the contrary, focuses on ruins as cultural artefacts and employs them as part of an exercise in environmental imagination, thereby stressing their narrative and theoretical potential in the understanding of the current environmental crisis. For this reason, real-life ruins and ruined spaces will be focused on much less than a wide variety of sources from different creative realms: non-fiction works and photography, science fiction and horror cinema, and twentieth-century fiction and political discourses. As wide as this selection is, it is not arbitrary. On the contrary, it is instrumental to highlighting the ubiquity of ruins in present-day ecological texts, as well as the importance of fictional works in shaping the environmental imagination. Discussing literary works and movies side to side with photography and non-fictional texts does not imply commenting on the fictional dimension of the latter, but rather on the power and potential of the former when it comes to address current ecological crises. It should be noted, finally, that the corpus gathered here is only partial, as seems to be inevitable when addressing such a vast and multifarious topic. Like all studies about ruination, this one, too, is necessarily unsystematic: the texts and visual elements I analyse are truly fragments shored against our ruins, to paraphrase T.S. Eliot.

This Element, in other words, is not concerned with the usual questions about ruins, which Zoltán Somhegyi aptly summarizes:

> Is it not strange that we are so delighted to see something dying, destroyed, and/or still in the process of being destroyed, when in other cases we look for the pristine and harmonious? ...What do we like in ruins? Why are we attracted to them, and how do we possibly define the elements of the architectural decay that accounts for the curious presence of ruins? (2020, 4)

That we like ruins, and that we like them so much that they are seemingly everywhere in our culture, is the starting point of this Element. The questions we intend to answer are: Why are ruins such an essential component of contemporary environmental imagination? What do ruins have to tell us about the present and the future of our relationship with the planet?

This Element is divided into four sections. Section 1 discusses the cultural genealogy of contemporary ruins, and their relevance to present-day ecological thought. Eighteenth- and nineteenth-century ruins offered viewers a vision of destruction that, in keeping with theorizations of the Romantic sublime, served as a terrible spectacle viewed from a safe distance – a tendency echoed in today's proliferation of 'dark tourism'. However, unlike their historical antecedents, contemporary representations of ruins consistently indulge in the decay of known or even intimate spaces (frequently immortalized by urbex photography and reportage), thereby reflecting an age of ecological precarity that involves every aspect of human life. The section shows how this tendency is connected to the growing instability of the planet's climate.

Section 2 focuses on an essential constituent of the imagination of ruins, and an especially prolific one in environmental terms: ruins as a space of encounter with non-human otherness, in contrast to traditional representations of ruins. The deep chronology evoked by traditional ruins, which facilitated a rumination on the passing of time and the inevitable fall of all civilizations, is extended indefinitely in the representations of contemporary ruins, which force viewers to confront vast, inhuman timescales that extend far beyond those of traditional ruins – not for centuries or millennia, but for hundreds of thousands of years. Building on the reading of ruins by Georg Simmel, the section discusses a classic of environmental non-fiction, *The World Without Us* (2007) by Alan Weisman, together with the sci-fi tv series *The Last of Us* (2023).

Section 3 takes into account a privileged subject in contemporary representations of ruins, the city of Detroit, whose progressive urban decay, due to a combination of infrastructural collapse and de-industrialization, has become the epitome of mournful ruminations on the decline of the American empire, even in official contexts. Detroit's ruins have been metabolized in our imagery to such an extent that they can function as the backdrop for horror movies like *Only Lovers Left Alive* (2013), *It Follows* (2014), and *Don't Breathe* (2016), repurposing the Gothic component of ruins – with the crucial difference that here vampires and monsters do not find refuge among the derelict remnants of a long-gone world, but in ordinary houses and buildings, such as can be found in most American towns. This spectral take on a post-industrial environment is also reflected in the work of photographers Andrew Moore, Yves Marchand, and Romain Meffre, whose depictions of ruined areas of Detroit reflect and adjourn Romantic and Gothic aesthetics.

Finally, Section 4 focuses on the crucial ambiguity of ruins in contemporary political and ecological discourses, especially in relation to nostalgia. In some environmentalist rhetoric, ruins become a space of openness, rewilding, and coexistence: once the human species has retreated, nature can flourish in the abandoned spaces left behind. Other discussions of ruins insist on their nostalgic function, as remnants of a past of greatness, making them a symbol of regressive nostalgia. Moreover, ruins (and especially those of malls and other spaces of consumerism) can function both as a symbol of the caducity of capitalist culture and as a re-semantization of the non-places of capitalism into spaces that are inherently imbued with history. Through a consideration of works like *Blade Runner 2049* (2017), and the 'semiotic ghosts' of William Gibson's 'The Gernsback Continuum' (1981), the section addresses the 'hauntological capacities' (Miller 2023, 1) of ruins, meaning their capacity to signify many things and intersect many temporal planes at once, and thereby simultaneously open up and preclude new environmental futures.

One thing needs to be added before moving on. A word will recur quite frequently in this Element, and indeed already has: 'nature', along with the adjective 'natural'. I am fully aware of the complications associated with this term, and of the fact that it is a very loaded one: I know that 'nature', very much like wilderness (Cronon 1996), is a cultural construction. Yet, the idea of a 'nature' that is external to the human world, to which culture (or 'spirit', as we will see) is in opposition, has been a pervasive feature of Western thought, and it still is a commonplace in many manifestations of our culture. Since this Element deals mostly with cultural objects, rather than concepts, I will use the term 'nature' to identify the polar opposition between these objects ('nature' and 'spirit'), rather than as something that actually exists as a unified agency outside ourselves. On the contrary, this oppositional view will be countered by the very discussion of ruins I am proposing. Similarly, another word that I will be employing often is intrinsically polysemic: 'Anthropocene'. It should be pointed out that I do not use this term to refer to the hypothesized geological epoch, but rather in its cultural sense – as a narrative framework, in other words, to understand the interrelatedness of seemingly separated ecological issues in contemporary global ecosystems. I also favour 'Anthropocene' to other proposed terms ('Capitalocene', 'Plantationocene', 'Petrocene'), including some I will use in this Element ('Wasteocene'), because of its comprehensiveness and capability of functioning as an umbrella term that includes the issues highlighted by these other categories.

1 A New *Ruinenlust*

1.1 A Matter of Terminology, or, Is There Such Thing as a Contemporary Ruin?

In Chapter XX of *Middlemarch*, George Eliot's historical novel published between 1871 and 1872, Dorothea Brooke and her husband, Reverend Casaubon, visit Rome on their honeymoon. Casaubon has chosen that destination in order to merge pleasure and work, as he is committed to the composition of a book systematizing antiquarian lore, titled *The Key to All Mythologies*. Alone in Rome while her husband is busy doing research, and filled with ambivalent emotions about her relationship with an older man of phlegmatic nature, Dorothea finds herself filled with a strange sadness, to which the surroundings greatly contribute. The ruined scenery of Rome has a powerful effect on the senses of an intellectual woman like Dorothea, whose stay in Italy is not motivated by the social networking in which most of her peers indulge, but by the higher purpose of helping her husband with his book:

> The weight of unintelligible Rome might lie easily on bright nymphs to whom it formed a background for the brilliant picnic of Anglo-foreign society; but Dorothea had no such defence against deep impressions. Ruins and basilicas, palaces and colossi, set in the midst of a sordid present, where all that was living and warm-blooded seemed sunk in the deep degeneracy of a superstition divorced from reverence; the dimmer but yet eager Titanic life gazing and struggling on walls and ceilings; the long vistas of white forms whose marble eyes seemed to hold the monotonous light of an alien world: all this vast wreck of ambitious ideals, sensuous and spiritual, mixed confusedly with the signs of breathing forgetfulness and degradation, at first jarred her as with an electric shock, and then urged themselves on her with that ache belonging to a glut of confused ideas which check the flow of emotion. (2000, 124)

Dorothea's reaction to the sight of classical and Christian ruins in Rome sums up a long-standing tendency in relation to these cultural artefacts: for over a century, the European imagination has used the imagery of ruins as counterpoints to modernity, remnants of a long-forgotten past that stand as a memento of the passing of time and the perishability and transitory nature of all human things. In Dorothea's eyes, ruins are vast, immobile, and noble, in contrast to the degeneracy of the present (and, more specifically, of Italy, from the perspective of a British Grand Tourist); yet, they are also a 'vast wreck', whose nobility and grandeur are not enough to save them from the destruction of time.

Ruins have played a pivotal role in the imagination of modernity: indeed, they appear to have been a constant obsession of modern intellectuals, as if modernity itself could only be defined in opposition to the remnants of the past. The discovery of the lost city of Pompeii in the eighteenth century prompted a melancholic enthusiasm for the subject of ruins across all Europe, as can be seen from even the vaguest survey of artistic products from the period: from Giovanni Battista Piranesi's hallucinatory prisons and capricci to Friedrich's sombre remnants of buildings of old; to the ubiquity of ruins in the Gothic novel, including in their titles, as in *The Ruins of Rigonda; or The Homicidal Father* (1808), *The Ruins of Tivoli* (1810) and *The Ruins of Selinunti or, The Val de Mazzara* (1813) (Wagner 2020, 67–68); to poetry about ruins, both in the work of graveyard poets like Thomas Warton and in that of Romantics like the Italian Giacomo Leopardi; to the use of ruins in political discourse, as in the case of Volney's *Les Ruines, ou Méditation sur les Révolutions des Empires* (1791; a book avidly read by the Creature of Mary Shelley's *Frankenstein*, 1818), and in Hubert Robert's 1796 painting *View of the Grande Galerie of the Louvre in*

Ruins, in which the depiction of the destroyed Louvre hints at the excesses of revolutionary activities (Ibata 2018, 204; see also Hell 2010). In that period, ruins seem to be discussed in all fields of human activity, from the art of vegetal cultivation and arrangement (as in *Observations on Modern Gardening* by Thomas Whately, 1770) to the history of humankind and its position in the world. Denis Diderot, himself a theorizer of the 'poetics of ruins', famously commented: 'the ideas ruins evoke in me are grand. ...In this vast, solitary, deserted sanctuary, I hear nothing, I'm isolated from all life's difficulties. No one hurries me along and no one is within earshot; I can speak to myself out loud, give voice to my afflictions and shed tears without restraint' (in Dillon 2011, 22).

This widespread fascination with ruins, which originated in the late eighteenth century, has been called *Ruinenlust* (quite literally 'ruin lust'), a cultural feeling that appears to have found renewed importance in the contemporary world. Yet, the ruin lust of the Romantics was mostly directed towards the ruins of ancient, nearly forgotten pasts (the 'basilicas, palaces and colossi' Dorothea contemplates in Rome); what we experience today is a ruin lust for remnants of our present. Talking about present ruins, however, calls into question the very definition of the term, and implies what Julia Hell and Andrea Schönle call the 'semantic instability of the ruin' (2010, 6): What is a ruin, if not something that 'seems to have lost its function or meaning in the present, while retaining a suggestive, unstable semantic potential' (6)? Is an unused building a ruin, even if it is not in decay? What about a decayed, but monumentalized, building? Is a preserved ruin an *authentic* ruin, or is the act of preservation contrary to the notion of ruination itself? The Colosseum in Rome is a ruin, in the sense that it is a partially collapsed building that has lost its original function, but it is also a carefully tended and polished monument, resulting in the loss of those elements of decay traditionally associated with ruins: in this sense, it could be argued that, despite being one of the epitomes of ruin lust in the past, the Colosseum today is less of a ruin than, say, an abandoned semi-detached house. As Dora Apel points out, 'the classical ruin has already reached its absolute form as an aesthetic artifact, defining its status as a ruin, and its preservation in this state is enforced and maintained by the guardians of the ruins'; on the contrary, the contemporary ruin 'is in a continuous state of flux' (2015, 12–13), a space of disorder rather than peace – something we will see in greater detail in the next section.

In texts associated with traditional *Ruinenlust*, ruins were seen mostly as something exotic: remnants of a distant past, but also (as was the case for the British and German tourists travelling through Italy) belonging to a geographic otherness. On the contrary, today's ruin lust is focused mostly on spaces and objects that belong to us: even when a spatial and cultural movement is involved, what we witness is still an everyday life only slightly different from our own. Slightly different, and yet already transmuted into something profoundly alien, as Tim Edensor notes: ruins 'are potential sites for a range of social activities which differ from those usually accorded preferential status in the city' (2005, 33). In a deeply estranging twist, when they become ruins, buildings lose their original functions but acquire new ones. If, as Apel argues, 'distancing is what facilitates a sense of political and cultural superiority over the disaster of ruination' (2015, 15), ruins of the present offer a much uncannier sight. They present us not with an abstract rumination on the perishability of human things but with the very tangible destruction of the world around us.

Unlike Dorothea, I do not need to travel far to see ruins: if I open one of the social media apps on my phone and search for the hashtag 'urbex', ruins from all around the world appear on the screen, side to side as in a Baroque capriccio (see Figures 2 and 3). 'Urbex' refers to 'the activity of exploring human-made structures and environments in the twenty-first century' (Bingham 2020, 4) – a widespread practice that has gathered a vast community of participants all around the globe, having originally emerged around the online presence of Jeff Chapman in the mid-1990s. Based in Toronto, Chapman was among the first to extensively document his urban exploration (a term he coined), which he also described in the posthumous book *Access All Areas: A User's Guide to the Art of Urban Exploration* (2005). As we will see later on when discussing the case of Detroit, many forms of the modern-day fascination with ruins – and urbex is no exception – have been accused of being 'ruin porn', which is to say, an exploitative exhibition of ruins for aesthetic purposes that ignores the historical depths of such ruins and the lives of the people associated with them (Dobraszczyk 2015, 13–14).

Clearly, there are still ruins in the present that retain an exceptional character: the ruins resulting from wars across the globe, from Ukraine to Gaza, from Iraq to Sudan; the ruins of terrorist violence, like the images of the crumbled Twin Towers after the 9/11 attacks; or, partially, the ruins of natural or human-made disasters, as in the abandoned cities of Chernobyl and Fukushima. Such images do not have the same value, in our culture, as a ruined, abandoned condo in the suburbs of our hometown. Yet, the vast majority of urbex websites and accounts are devoted, as the name suggests, to the ruins of domestic and private buildings scattered on the margins of our cities: our interest appears to have shifted from the monumental, exotic, exceptional ruins of the past to those that most closely resemble our own way of life and the spaces we encounter (and after all, what were the ruins of Kharkiv, Gaza, and Chernobyl, if not houses and public spaces similar to the ones we inhabit every day? What did the Twin Towers contain, if

Figure 2 Screenshot of the Instagram's 'For you' page with the search words 'Urban exploration'.

not offices more or less like the ones in which we work?). Of course, some examples of urbex photography are exceptionally traditional in their scope and play extensively on eighteenth- and nineteenth-century architecture, thereby covering the ruination of structures built in the very age that saw the rise of ruin lust. The work of Sven Fennema, for instance, mostly features scenographic ruins of (neo)gothic palaces from all around Europe (as in the *Forgotten Splendor* series) or even cemeteries (*Memento*, 2022), and two of his books are titled *Nostalgia* (2015) and *Melancholia* (2018), two feelings traditionally associated with ruins. Fennema, like many urbex documenters, exploits the grandeur of ruins as an easy source of aesthetic pleasure, but does not investigate their meaning and function in today's world. Most other urbex photographers, however, tend to focus on everyday spaces and objects: Jason Lanier portrays resorts and hotels, asylums

Figure 3 Marco Ricci, *A Classical Landscape with Ruins*, 1725. Public domain (Wikicommons).

and amusements parks, while Shane Thoms documents mundane locations in Japan, Australia, and North America, or the ghost district near Ordos in Northern China – a massive real-estate project that was never inhabited.

As Susan Stewart notes, the evolution of the eighteenth century's 'pleasure for ruins' (or Diderot's 'poetics of ruins') into present-day 'ruin porn' depends on the widespread presence of photography in everyday life, but also on the peculiar, albeit vague, meaning that most of us ascribe to ruins: 'the immediate testimony of the photograph bears witness to what cannot be known as presence – such erupting violence, on the one hand, or the precarious and unstable conditions of extant ruined forms, on the other' (Stewart 2020, 5). Precariousness, violence, instability, all these elements are core constituents of the conceptualization of ruins, and are also central in contemporary theorizations of the Anthropocene. Throughout this Element, we shall see how ruins are employed in contemporary environmental discourse to visualize a violence that is often too oblique and subtle to be understood until it explodes in sudden bursts, but also as reminders of the power of non-human agencies.

1.2 Dread at a Safe Distance: Ruins, the Sublime, and the Anthropocene

One aesthetic concept has been consistently associated with ruins: that of the sublime. Eighteenth-century theorists of this aesthetic concept adapted

Longinus' discussion of the sublime in the context of natural scenery to their own growing interest (typical of the Romantic period) in nature and nature writing (Ibata 2018, 31). The sublime is connected with transcendence, with the perception of something beyond human capabilities and forces; therefore, it 'marks the limits of reason and expression together with a sense of what might lie beyond these limits' (Shaw 2006, 2). It is true that authors like Edmund Burke and Immanuel Kant, as well as other theorists of the sublime, tend to discuss it mostly in relation to natural elements and their artistic reproduction (see Doran 2015); yet, they do so in terms that can be extended to ruins and ruination. For instance, Kant lists as examples of the sublime 'the sight of a mountain whose snow-covered peaks arise above the clouds, the description of a raging storm, or the depiction of the kingdom of hell by Milton, . . . lofty oaks and lonely shadows in sacred groves' (2011, 14–16): compared to the beautiful, the sublime elicits a strong impression, often connected with a sense of dread. The feeling of the sublime, Kant continues, 'is sometimes accompanied with some dread or even melancholy, in some cases merely with quiet admiration and in yet others with a beauty spread over a sublime prospect' – distinctions that correspond to 'the terrifying sublime, . . . the noble, and . . . the magnificent', respectively (2011, 16). The sublime derives its force from being vaster and wider than human senses: 'the sublime must always be large', argues Kant; 'a great height is just as sublime as a great depth' (2011, 17). This is true even on a chronological scale, as long as it exceeds human perception: 'a long duration is sublime. If it is of time past, it is noble; if it is projected forth into an unforeseeable future, then there is something terrifying in it. An edifice from the most distant antiquity is worthy of honor' (2011, 18).

As this last remark attests, in Kant's view a ruined edifice can elicit a sense of the sublime. Burke is even more explicit, as he identifies the sublime with 'the ideas of pain and danger', or, in other words,

> whatever is in any sort terrible, or is conversant about terrible objects, or operates in a manner analogous to terror, is a source of the sublime; that is, it is productive of the strongest emotion which the mind is capable of feeling. . . . When danger or pain press too nearly, they are incapable of giving any delight, and are simply terrible; but at certain distances, and with certain modifications, they may be, and they are delightful, as we every day experience. (1998, 36)

The sublime, then, is the terrible at a distance: precisely the kind of feeling that ruins evoke. Ruins present the fall of a civilization (a beloved subject of one of the most popular Romantic painters of the Romantic era, John Martin), but this fall is located in the past, at a safe distance from the viewer. For tourists like Dorothea, the multilayered ruins of Rome represent a way of experiencing the melancholy associated with the passing of time without having to mourn the loss of something known and loved. Andrew F. Wood argues that ruins do not belong to the sublime, as 'we do not read a ruin through some pre-linguistic understanding', which is essential to the sublime (2021, 31). Ruins are, rather, picturesque, as historically theorized by William Gilpin (Somhegyi 2020, 15–16): 'while ruins possess the ability to rouse feelings of contemplative dread and the realization of one's mortality, they do not reside beyond the scope of human agency' (Wood 2021, 31). This is not entirely false: clearly, ruins are not external to the human the way a glacier or a thunderstorm are. Yet, ruins possess power precisely because they are crossed and intersected by agencies beyond the human: the very process of ruination is caused by, and epitomizes, such agencies, and ruins themselves are symbols of the activity of powers far greater and vaster, and more pervasive, than humanity, that play out on timescales that exceed the duration of human lives and societies.

Despite their being seldom discussed in Burke and Kant, 'from the beginning of the eighteenth century, ruins, vestiges of the past and architectural fragments became an essential feature of the British cultural imaginary and a recurrent topos in the arts' (Ibata 2018, 203). This fascination was encouraged by continuous archaeological discoveries of ruins, in Italy and the rest of Europe, most importantly at the sites of Pompeii and Herculaneum. While 'the sublime potential of ruins and ancient edifices was not immediately made evident', the development of Romantic aesthetics and Gothic fiction developed this connection: in France, it led to the development of 'the "sentiment des ruines" ...: a pleasing form of melancholy or nostalgia, leading to a philosophical meditation about the passing of time and the transience of human inscription. In Britain, it gave rise to a long-lasting taste for picturesque ruins' (Ibata 2018, 206–7). It is no coincidence that theorizations of the sublime followed the Lisbon earthquake of 1755. As Dora Apel points out, 'the Lisbon earthquake serves as a prototype for the modern postapocalyptic ruin imaginary and the aesthetic of the sublime' (2015, 18; see also Regier 2010).

In this sense, the tendency to represent ruins of one's present, discussed in the previous section, is not unprecedented. Among the few explicit discussions of ruins Burke offers, for instance, one in particular has endured, the image of the destruction of London (by an earthquake, as had been the case for Lisbon too):

> This noble capital, the pride of England and of Europe, I believe no man is so strangely wicked as to desire to see destroyed by a conflagration or an earthquake, though he should be removed himself to the greatest distance from the danger. But suppose such a fatal accident to have happened, what numbers from all parts would croud to behold the ruins, and amongst them many who would have been content never to have seen London in its glory? (1998, 44)

This image has been famously reprised many times, from Mary Wollstonecraft Shelley's *The Last Man* (1826) to the final engraving of Gustave Doré's illustrations for Blanchard Jerrold's *London: A Pilgrimage* (1872). In Jerrold and Doré, the visitor pondering the ruins of London is a New Zealander, occupying the same position as the Grand Tourists faced with the ruins of distant exotic countries (Dobraszczyk 2015, 23). In Burke's case, the representation of London in ruins serves to highlight the importance of distance and sympathy in the enjoyment of the terrible that elicits a sense of the sublime: 'it is absolutely necessary', Burke continues, 'my life should be out of any imminent hazard before I can take a delight in the sufferings of others, real or imaginary, or indeed in any thing else from any cause whatsoever' (1998, 44). The destruction of London is a terrible catastrophe, akin to one that had recently struck another European capital, but this catastrophe is also a purely hypothetical one, displaced in the distant future, thus allowing the mind to take pleasure in it without really being concerned by the suffering involved in a real tragedy. Similarly, Lord Byron opens his famous 'Ode on Venice' (1819) with an apocalyptic image of the city devoured by the rising seas:

> Oh Venice! Venice! when thy marble walls
> Are level with the waters, there shall be
> A cry of nations o'er thy sunken halls,
> A loud lament along the sweeping sea! (vv. 1–4)

This depiction of Venice in ruins, however, has little to do with the Venetian ecosystem, but rather serves to comment on the contemporary decay of the city, whose political independence was brought to an end a few years previous by Napoleon's ruthless political calculus: 'Thirteen hundred years / of wealth and glory turned to dust and tears' (vv. 15–16). In the past, both politically and culturally, images of contemporary buildings and cities in ruins have fuelled anxieties about societal decline and, in the case of London, reverse colonization.

The concept of the sublime has been extensively mobilized,[3] in recent years, to address the environmental changes of the Anthropocene, as well as the changes in our relationship with the environment and the idea of nature. Unlike Burke's ruined London, in the Anthropocene, environmental catastrophes are not a distant hypothesis, but rather something that is occurring in many areas of the planet at an increasing rate. Representing the present in ruins is no longer a tool to reflect on a possibility, but rather a means of highlighting an ongoing process. The erosion of boundaries between nature and culture has

---

[3] For an overview, see Ray 13–15. Besides the sources directly quoted here, see Hitt 1999; Caracciolo 2021; Borsari 2022. See also the special issue of *Ecozon@* on 'Anthropocene sublimes', 16(1), 2025.

done away with that safe distance that made the enjoyment of the Romantic sublime possible in the first place: despite all its inherent inequalities, the warming the planet is experiencing is *global* and the product of human activities. As Bruno Latour has argued, the traditional understanding of the sublime 'has evaporated as soon as we are no longer taken as those puny humans overpowered by "nature" but, on the contrary, as a collective giant that, in terms of terawatts, has scaled up so much that it has become the main geological force shaping the Earth' (Latour 2011, 3). Traditional accounts of the sublime focusing on an external nature as an entity separated from humanity no longer apply to the Anthropocene; yet, 'a new planetary context of terror is emerging' (Ray 2020, 2), a context that encourages a shift from a transcendent understanding of the sublime to one that includes the interaction of human and non-human forces – an interaction that is central in the process of ruination. Contemporary representations of ruins that mostly focus on the ruins of the present and not the past, of the domestic and not the exceptional, reflect this change in perspective and reduce the safe distance that guaranteed the aesthetic enjoyment of the Romantic sublime.

Indeed, it might be argued, as Latour in some ways did, that in today's world there is no longer room for the sublime, that there are few things that escape or exceed human control, and that there are fewer and fewer inaccessible spaces that might somehow elicit our sense of wonder (Brady 2012, 173–4). While Giacomo Leopardi's 'Dialogue between Nature and an Icelander' (1835) is set in Africa, by making his protagonist an Icelander the author is evoking the island's distant and harsh landscapes, which in the minds of his readers could function as an image of the inhuman forces at play in the natural world, and the vast and uncaring realms of matter outside human control. Today, however, Iceland is one of the world's most popular tourist destinations, easily accessible by flight and extensively explored, its most dangerous locations having become a fashionable source of entertainment. The feeling of powerlessness and awe experienced by Victor Frankenstein when faced with the Alpine landscape could hardly be experienced today (the Alps are, after all, the most anthropized mountains in the world), or has, at least, been transformed into a commodified experience. The sublime as theorized by Kant and Burke only partially applies to today's environments, or has to be directed towards something even more external, like the depths of outer space. Yet, the sublime is still present in a different form, when we are confronted not with the domesticated version of the natural world, as envisioned by the Romantics, but rather by the non-human agencies at play in the Anthropocene and the way in which they are elicited by human forces. The hole in the ozone layer or the changes to the Gulf Stream are massive, potentially catastrophic phenomena that could have dreadful effects on human civilization and that are not the product of natural forces, but rather of human activities.

The feeling of the sublime applies when we are faced with the manifestations of natural violence and agency at play in the Anthropocene – manifestations that are inextricably tied to human activity. Rather than pristine landscapes, today the feeling of the sublime is elicited by the action of natural forces (geological, biological, and atmospheric) against the forms and symbols of human culture. Yet, unlike Lisbon's earthquake, these forces no longer seem external to humanity, but are rather influenced by anthropogenic climate and environmental change. This is why ruins are perhaps more important to the Anthropocene sublime than to the Romantic sublime: because they prove that the natural world is not an external otherness, vast and powerful but separated from us, whose activity (as in the case of an earthquake or an eruption) is sudden and temporary, but rather something that is always present and always acting in the world. Ruins reduce the distance that we have put between ourselves and the natural world, and function as a warning about the alienated relationship between contemporary societies and non-human life. The fires in Los Angeles, the floods in Emilia-Romagna, hurricane Helene in North Carolina, these natural disasters, heavily influenced by the instabilities of climate change and excesses in urbanization, are the spectacle that gives rise to the sublime today, together with the countless ruins they leave in their wake.

1.3 Touring Destruction: The Spectacle of Ruins

In keeping with Kant's claim that 'the sublime must always be large', theorizers of the conceptual consequences of the Anthropocene framework have pointed out that the effects of climate change defy human temporalities and spatial understanding. Timothy Morton employs the notion of non-locality to describe climate change, meaning that its specific manifestations do not exhaust or add up to it as a phenomenon (2013, 1), while Rob Nixon describes Anthropocenic violence as a slow violence, occurring at a pace that we usually do not associate with violence at all (2011, 2). The violence of the Anthropocene sublime is no longer that which elicited the imagination of the Romantics (the sudden, devastating earthquake), but rather a slow process, often invisible, that only occasionally manifests in violent outbursts: a process of penetration, erosion, and decay that is eloquently encapsulated in the form of the ruin. Ruins provide a physical, tangible manifestation of Anthropocenic violence, thus forcing viewers to confront the deep chronologies of environmental history, as well as the complexity of its unfolding – elements that were central to Kant's discussion of the sublime, but that take on a new meaning in the inhuman chronologies of the Anthropocene. A negative ecology, in this sense, is also one that needs to confront the hidden violence at play in familiar landscapes.

Dora Apel correctly points to the connection between the fascination with ruins and the anxiety of decline: 'the anxiety of decline feeds an enormous appetite for ruin imagery. ... As fears of decline grow, the threshold for compensatory aesthetic pleasure also grows higher, requiring more expressions of ruin and disaster to be mentally mastered in order to achieve a sense of safety' (2015, 10). We have observed this in our discussion of the occasional appearance of ruins of the present in the Romantic and Gothic imagination as a means of representing and exorcizing the fear of decay and reverse colonization. However, it also applies to the present, considering the widespread presence of eco-anxiety in the public conscience. In an age that is increasingly (and justifiably) preoccupied with the endangered status of the planet's ecosystems and the changes in the global climate, and in which these preoccupations have started to colonize the mental space of everyday life, we resort to ruins as a means of exorcizing the dangers of the future. By constantly bringing such destruction before our eyes, we try to escape it.

As we have seen in the case of urbex, contemporary culture is not at all reluctant to exhibit its own fascination with disaster and decay. This can easily be seen in another increasingly widespread phenomenon: what is usually called 'dark tourism', a term that refers to the 'presentation and consumption (by visitors) of real and commodified death and disaster sites' (Foley and Lennon 1996, 198; see also Light 2017). Popular sites for dark tourism include, for instance, prisons and torture chambers; the locations of famous murders, from the site of John Fitzgerald Kennedy's assassination to the places where Jeffrey Dahmer found, killed, and ate his victims; and, inevitably, places where disasters occurred. It seems quite clear, then, that a central component of dark tourism is the presence of ruins, which provide tourists with the opportunity to see with their own eyes destroyed spaces immortalized in the news, as in the cases of Chernobyl and Fukushima. TripAdvisor offers no less than twenty-five guided tours of Chernobyl and Pripyat, which give visitors the chance to 'see where history unfolded' and 'to take plenty of photos', and 'even [to] have lunch at the workers' canteen'.[4] If ruins are sublime inasmuch they make viewers feel wonder in relation to the vast, inhuman processes at play in their creation, few places could prove more suitable than cities abandoned after nuclear disasters. At the same time, the spaces explored in contemporary ruin tourism are intrinsically mundane (e.g., the workers' canteen); they are not

---

[4] www.tripadvisor.com/AttractionProductReview-g294474-d19645523-Chernobyl
_Tour_with_Gift-Kyiv.html.

monumental but are rendered uncanny by the catastrophe that occurred there: they mirror the known spaces we inhabit, which are subject to the same attritional and invisible violence and the same constant danger that, in these cases, have so eloquently manifested themselves.

As Martini and Sharma note, 'the potential for sublime experiences of a post-disaster landscape is immensely commodifiable for tourism purposes because of the fascination towards dark and apocalyptic fantasies' (2022, 10). It is fitting, in this sense, that contemporary tourism's historical roots can be found in the eighteenth-century Grand Tour – itself a practice profoundly centred around ruins. Visiting such sites offers tourists the possibility of almost living the disaster themselves by encountering the ruins it left behind. Compared to more traditional sites of disaster tourism, such as Pompeii (Skinner 2018), which contributed to prompting an obsession with ruins in eighteenth-century Europe, Fukushima offers something more: not just the spectacle of destruction due to natural causes but also a human-made spectacle that evokes the 'nuclear sublime' (Ferguson 1984; Goatcher and Brunsden 2011; Masco 2021). As in the case of Chernobyl, visiting sites of nuclear disasters allows tourists to immerse themselves in a landscape, and relive an event, that has been immortalized in countless works of fiction about atomic holocausts and the end of the world – and the tragic effect of these disasters is enhanced by this continuous fictional rumination. Again, these are tendencies that confirm what we suggested earlier: dark tourism is a morbid way of confronting one's fears about decline and death, destruction and violence; a means of soothing these anxieties by experiencing them in a safe environment.

Yet, the disaster of Fukushima was not just an accident, but rather the lethal combination of natural forces and human miscalculations. It was caused by a tsunami that inundated a nuclear power plant, causing a fallout that rendered the area uninhabitable, and therefore calls into question humanity's inability to control the forces it summons. Moreover, the disaster also questions the decision to place such infrastructure in unstable places, which seems to demonstrate a blindness to the destructive power of the natural world. While we are led to believe that certain infrastructure essential to our society, and specifically nuclear infrastructure, is immune to dangers and errors, Fukushima proved that basic miscalculation by human actors can occur even in such cases, and with deadly consequences. Perhaps even more than the disaster in Chernobyl, the Fukushima disaster encapsulates the contradictions of human development in the Anthropocene, when inhuman powers are exploited only to be turned into sources of danger, disease, and death when they become uncontrollable. The Anthropocene and the atomic energy industrial complex (both 'industrially manufactured existential dangers', to reprise the words of Joseph Masco; in Mariani 2022, 184) are closely intertwined: nuclear isotopes are one of the geological markers of the Anthropocene (Zalasiewicz et al. 2008), while the development of nuclear technology is closely related to the development of ecology itself. Nuclear isotopes introduced into ecosystems made it possible to visualize relationships between natural elements that had only been hypothesized (Hurley 2020, 10), while the programme Atoms for Peace contributed to financing ecological research (2020, 161); in this sense, environmental studies in the second half of the twentieth century have provided 'cover for many of the most appalling acts of violence performed by the nuclear complex' and 'some of the first irrefutable evidence that the nuclear complex was damaging the planet and its inhabitants in ways that might be uncontrollable and irreversible' (2020, 161).

Like urbex, dark tourism could easily fall under the label of ruin porn (even more so, in fact, considering the non-profit nature of urban exploration): an exploitative relationship with sites of disaster that commodify individual and ecosystemic tragedies as a source of cheap thrills. Not all inquiries into disasters, however, are exploitative, even when they adhere to the form of the reportage. William T. Vollmann's *Into the Forbidden Zone: A Trip through Hell and High Water in Post-earthquake Japan* (2011), later included in an expanded version in the first volume of *Carbon Ideologies* (*No Immediate Danger*; 2018), is an exploration of post-disaster Fukushima. Vollmann, a celebrated fiction writer (he was awarded the National Book Award for *Europe Central*, 2005), has also extensively engaged in reportage from all around the world, often in dangerous situations, from Afghanistan to the Balkans, from Cambodia to the Arctic Circle. His peregrination in post-disaster Fukushima is characterized by the observation of the visible remnants of the disaster, in the forms of ruins, and a recording of the invisible peril still at large in the environment, radiation – all of which constitute the ruins of everyday spaces, not famous monuments.

In Fukushima, Vollmann brings a Geiger counter, allowing him to record and keep track of the radiation level in the city (the first section of the book is eloquently titled 'Picaresque Wanderings of a Dosimeter'). The Geiger counter is one of the ways in which Vollmann tries to make visible something that is not, like radioactivity. The other tool Vollmann employs are photographs: as is often the case in his books, *Into the Forbidden Zone* (and even more so *Carbon Ideologies*) is filled with pictures, taken by Vollmann himself, not dissimilarly from what Peter Goin did in the photobook *Nuclear Landscapes*, 1991 (see Glotfelty 2014). The issue of visibility is central in these two works by Vollmann, and is one of the crucial concerns of discourses about pollution and environmental degradation. In line with the idea of Anthropocene violence as a 'slow violence', as theorized by Rob Nixon, Jessica Hurley wonders how to make visible 'the connections between tumors and the factory that closed down two generations ago, between what we know of bioaccumulation and what we feel when we look at a carrot' (2020, 164–5). For Vollmann, these connections can be suggested by individual stories and images of the people and spaces involved; as he argues in the introductory pages of *No Immediate Danger*, 'to our species ... seeing was believing. The unseeable might require numbers to gain credence, as was the case with radiation, which all too many of the Japanese I met at Fukushima consoled themselves was invisible' (2018a, 20).

Vollmann is thus an example of a 'sublime tourist' not because he visits ruined sites, but rather because ruins become in his writing a physical manifestation of the many, largely invisible non-human powers that human activity has unleashed. In his account of his visit to Fukushima, pictures of ruins are paired with descriptions of crumbled and fragmented spaces of everyday life:

> A fallen pine, cables, heaps of mud, bent pipes, metal grilles, fallen poles as thick as my shoulder, these sad and ugly objects varied themselves monotonously all the way to the mud horizon. On one side of the road the former fields were flooded with seawater. On the other, on the edge of streaming tidal flats which used to be rice fields, a two-story concrete house, windowless but seemingly intact, supported a second home that had been smashed up against it, the roof twisted like sections of ruined armor, both structures choked with rubbish. A detachment of goggled, web-belted, booted, camouflage-uniformed Self-Defense Forces from Hokkaido were dissecting the two houses in search of bodies. The slogan one often saw on their helmets was: 'Let's cheer up, Sendai!' (2018a, 268–9)

Here, Vollmann portrays the confusion that followed the natural disaster of the tsunami, by depicting an uninhabited, crumbled space where smashed and destroyed relics of human activity are invaded by eradicated trees and seawater. At the same time, however, Vollmann does not simply depict a landscape that has been destroyed by a natural disaster, as could have been the case in the context of Lisbon's earthquake, but one that has been poisoned by radiation, thus by human activity. Descriptions of the infected land abound:

> [T]he driver pointed out some nara trees (good for growing mushrooms, he said; a few days later, the news ... announced that mushrooms in a certain zone near the reactor could no longer be harvested, having exceeded the legal radiation limit). Nearly everywhere I looked in Ono there were small, square garden plots where vegetables were coming in, in neat rows, young and green; were they poisonous? The sun was strangely warm on my wrists, or perhaps they were tingling from the potassium iodide. (2018a, 311)

Ruined buildings are paired with the spectral scenery of irradiated vegetation, which poses a potential risk if consumed: Vollmann depicts a haunted landscape, apparently calm but ready to act against human bodies. This risk, and this kind of depiction, is not limited to nuclear radiation, however, as invisibility is one of the essential characters of most kinds of pollution. In volume two of *Carbon Ideologies* (*No Good Alternative*), Vollmann describes his visit to McDowell County in West Virginia, a former mining community and one of the United States' unhealthiest counties, as well as the county with the shortest life expectancy. When he discusses the risks connected to coal mining, such as the contaminated water supply, Vollmann uses pictures of ruined buildings in the area. Given the impossibility of portraying the invisible perils of polluted water, Vollmann resorts to showing the post-industrial ruins of the county, the abandoned houses and infrastructure. Ruins become the vector through which to visualize endangered ecosystems and environmental damage spanning several decades; a testimony not just of the perishability of the human world, as in traditional depictions of ruins, but also of the durability of its negative effects on the planet.

2 The World without Whom?

2.1 'Like Elements in Dreams': Creative Ruination

So far we have discussed the ruin as a symbol of destruction, proof of the capability of non-human elements to unmake the artefacts of human civilization – a capability, we should add, that is greatly enhanced, and rendered less predictable, by the turmoil of climate change. We have also discussed the semantic instability of ruins, whose meaning and (lack of) function is exclusively determined in relation to the society that interrogates them. Despite such semantic instability – or, rather, because of it – ruins are such eloquent symbols, signalling 'the impending breakdown of meaning and therefore foster[ing] intensive compensatory discursive activity' (Hell and Schönle 2010, 6). From an environmental perspective, ruins prompt reflections on both the deep temporality of the Anthropocene and the agency of matter. Representing present buildings and spaces as ruins means interrogating the forces that are at play in what is otherwise perceived as an anthropocentric world.

Ruins are proof of the intersection between human and non-human agencies, and of the ways in which human artefacts are absorbed and transformed by the non-human. According to Zoltán Somhegyi, ruins need to be functionless, meaning that to qualify as a ruin a building has to be unable 'to fulfil its original function' (2020, 6). Most importantly, at the core of the ruin there is an absence (2020, 8): the process of ruination empties a building of meaning and function, but this absence allows for the emergence of something else, for the introduction of a variety of agencies. A ruin is not created by absence per se, but by the activity of other forces, both inorganic and organic. The ruin, in other words, is not to be understood as an atemporal stillness, an object from times past that is now situated outside time; rather, it has to be seen as a continuous process. While traditional depictions of ruins associated them with the cessation of life, and therefore a sense of melancholic peace, contemporary depictions focus much more on the interplay of agencies active in the process of ruination.

The dynamic dimension of ruins is underlined by the fact that, as Susan Stewart suggests, 'the word *ruin* is both a noun and a verb' (2020, 1): it simultaneously refers to something fixed in time and the very process of producing that thing. The same ambiguity characterizes the word 'ruination', as Ann Laura Stoler points out: it means 'an act of ruining, a condition of being ruined, and a cause of it', therefore 'an *act* perpetrated, a *condition* to which one is subject, and a *cause* of loss' (2013, 11). According to Aleksandra Prica, decay is the central element of ruination: focusing on decay, rather than on the ruins as an object, means underlining the 'processuality' of ruins – decay 'makes abundantly clear that ruins are elements in a course of events that alter them' (2022, 7–9). From an environmental perspective, this ambiguity becomes particularly eloquent, as it conveys the ruination industrial modernity inflicts upon planetary ecosystems, but also the condition of these ecosystems, and the cause of their state.

In keeping with the notion of a negative ecology, ruins, in being a process rather than an object, stand for the disordered: not spaces from which life has disappeared, but rather spaces teeming with forms of life that we usually keep outside our houses, cities, societies, and cultures. Ruins, according to Tim Edensor, 'gain an aesthetic charge by virtue of this difference' from 'normative aesthetic orderings' (2005, 76). It is precisely this aesthetic charge that is captured by contemporary depictions of ruins, which portray the proliferation of life at the expense of human structures. In ruins, our aesthetic and cultural values are reframed: 'objects, textures and fragments fall out of their previously assigned contexts to recombine like elements in dreams, a random re-ordering which is determined by where things land or are thrown' (2005, 115). 'Like elements in dreams', this recalls the arteficial, yet suggestive, compository practice of the capriccio (a style of scenic painting that brought together buildings, monuments, and ruins from different parts of a city or country), but also the portentous ways in which a ruin is formed from elements that seem apparently unrelated and irreconcilable (and let us remember that the protagonist of Friedrich's view of Oybin monastery is 'the dreamer'). Different parts of buildings merge together, crumble, and are pulverized and destroyed by the weather, while at the same time new forms of life creep in from the outside, or from the margins of our houses, where we usually cannot, or refuse to, see them or make attempts to control them: insects, birds, small mammals, plants, fungi, and mould. To reprise Somhegyi, in the absence of human presence and functions, other forms and things can be found.

Given the extent to which so many portrayals of ruins are focused on tranquillity and an absence of life, it might seem counterintuitive to read them as cradles of life, deep intersections of non-human agencies. Yet, the crucial thing about ruins (both past and contemporary), which makes them especially important in today's ecological thought, is precisely that they only come to be as a result of the intervention of natural elements. This is also what leads to them being such an omnipresent symbol of ecological reflection. This interplay was clearly outlined by Georg Simmel in his short but influential essay 'The Ruin' [Die Ruine] (1911). Simmel notes that at the centre of ruins' aesthetic power stands the interaction of human and non-human forces: 'the ruin of a building ... means that where the work of art is dying, other forces and forms, those of nature, have grown; and that out of what art still lives in the ruin and what of nature already lives in it, there has emerged a new whole, a characteristic unity' (1958, 380). In the process of ruination, buildings and monuments find a 'new meaning', whose 'spiritual form [is comprehended] in a unity which is no longer grounded in human purposiveness but in that depth where human purposiveness and the working of non-conscious natural forces grow from their common root' (1958, 380).

Roman ruins, in Simmel's view, are often of little interest since 'one notices in them the destruction *by man*; for this contradicts the contrast between human work and the effect of *nature* on which rests the significance of the ruin as such' (1958, 380). It is not destruction in itself that is fascinating but the ways in which the process of ruination involves a variety of agencies, as if the retreat of humans leaves space for the intervention of other forces: 'it is the fascination of the ruin that here [human work] appears to us entirely as a product of nature. The same forces which give a mountain its shape through weathering, erosion, faulting, and the growth of vegetation, here do their work on old walls' (1958, 381). This last notion is interesting in light of the Anthropocene sublime: if we take into account Dipesh Chakrabarty's idea that in the Anthropocene humans moved from being a biological force to a geological one (2009, 207), Simmel's depiction of a human artefact being re-taken by (among others) geological forces is complicated by the transformation of the human species into just such a force – by its becoming, in other words, one of those very forces that 'give a mountain its shape'. Even more so than a 110 years ago, when Simmel was writing, contemporary ruins encapsulate the undeniable merging of human and non-human forces.

However, if ruination is the result of destructive forces, of a decay induced by non-human elements, it is also a *creative* process: through destruction, architectural objects ('the most sublime victory of the spirit over nature', according to Simmel; 1958, 379) are not annihilated, but turned into something different. The 'unique balance' of forces and elements central to architecture 'breaks' during the process of ruination, and 'merely natural forces begin to become master over the work of man' (Simmel 1958, 379); these natural forces start a new, creative process that uses human artefacts as their canvas. The fragments of other human artefacts (paintings, sculpture, literature) are not inherently as fascinating as a ruin; while their aesthetic power depends only on the extent to which something of the original work can be glimpsed in them, ruins are visually and conceptually interesting because something else is now at play (1958, 380). If, as Somhegyi argues, 'buildings are originally constructed "against" Nature', in the sense that they protect people from natural elements (2020, 4), ruination dissolves this boundary between nature and culture, internal and external, and pristine and artificial. Natural elements are what makes a ruin what it is, and this is the reason why, in traditional painting, ruins are so often inserted into natural landscapes (2020, 4–5).

Ruins, then, are an essentially anti-anthropocentric object in which the conceptual organization of the world is subverted, and 'the hierarchy of nature and spirit' that traditionally sees the spirit as the 'crowning element' and nature as the 'raw material' is reversed: what was raised by the spirit becomes the object of the same forces that form the contour of the mountain and the bank of the river (1958, 380). The process of ruination, in other words, suggests that 'nature has a never completely extinguished rightful claim to this work' (1958, 382) and therefore that the presumption that human life can be autonomous and separate from the non-human agencies of the world is false. It is not that these agencies are absent from our lives, but rather that the systems of life that our culture has envisioned tend to push them to the margins, to render them physically and culturally invisible. Infesting plants and invasive moulds and fungi are all omnipresent, yet hidden, in our environments: ruination creates a space in which they can re-emerge. The ruin is not an empty space, but one from which human life is progressively retreating – not empty, but emptier: 'the return of the agency of the wild, the role of plants and animals in producing space, becomes evident, transgressing the assignation of nature and underlining the threat posed by the ruin' (Edensor 2005, 47).

In this sense, ruins can be understood within the framework of waste – indeed, as part of what Marco Armiero has called the 'Wasteocene', a different label for the Anthropocene that shifts the attention to waste as an essential part of humanity's presence on the planet (including, of course, both physical waste and more invisible forms like CO_2). Central to the concept of waste, as in ruination, is the notion of a 'wasting relationship', involving the creation of an 'other' that is external to us, and thus less valuable (Armiero 2021, 2). This process of othering takes place both materially, in terms of a division between what is suitable for life and what is not, and among humans, as it creates a division between those who create waste and those who have to deal with it, dispose of it, and endure it. Othering, in relation to waste, means shipping it from richer countries to poorer ones, or relegating it to specific parts of nations, thereby creating unsanitary spaces, toxic areas, or endangered communities, like those documented by Vollmann in West Virginia. In relation to ruins, this othering concerns the process of ruination, which is to say, the momentary collapse of this separation between categories through the transformation of entire buildings, and the objects that populate them, into waste: in ruination, all elements acquire the same value, and non-human forces regain their agency ('in the ruin', Tim Edensor writes, 'all objects are equal, none assigned higher value than others, because they are all categorised as trash'; 2005, 100).

Very much like ruins, waste is a cultural concept before it is a physical status: as John Scanlan writes, garbage 'is the formlessness from which form takes flight' (2005, 14). What we throw away, in other words, defines who and what we are; we give meaning to the world by separating things from one another (2005, 15; see also Douglas 2001, 1–6). This is true in the case of ruins as well, as we have seen in relation to the 'semantic instability' of the word. A ruin is not necessarily useless, dangerous, or unpleasant, but is rather a space lacking societal recognition, something that has lost its function in the eyes of a culture, but that, precisely for this reason, can serve other functions and other entities. Ruins show us the arbitrariness of this process of othering, this division between ourselves and the other. Animals entering a ruined building, nesting there, nurturing communities and families, do not signal a violation of human space, but rather the lability of the distinction between 'us' as human animals and 'them' as the vast, undifferentiated mass of non-human animals to which our language confines them.

The status of ruin could be extended to other forms of waste that are not necessarily just architectonic. Landfills, for instance, are not simply collections of waste, but rather entire spaces informed and transformed by the process of creating waste, in which human artefacts are brought together and mutated by the action of non-human agencies, in a dynamic of decay that is essentially akin to the one at play in ruination (and besides landfills, this takes place in all the 'sacrifice zones', i.e. areas permanently altered by human-produced waste, deliberately engineered and left behind by contemporary industrial and farming practices). Like ruined buildings, landfills are human spaces that are crowded with abandoned human objects – objects that have lost their value, and that have therefore exited the coordinates of our culture and can become something else, thanks to the action of bacteria, mould, fungi, vegetation, and small animals. It is telling that, in Edward Burtynsky's pictures of landfills, these sites are rendered with the same larger-than-human proportions that we find in traditional depictions of ruins, with tyres and destroyed cars looming and twisting in menacing geometries, as distorted by rust as the buildings in Piranesi's work have been distorted by time. The sense of dread and oppression conveyed by Piranesi is similar to that which Burtynsky tries to convey in his alienating images of consumerism, featuring endless lines of tyres, cars, and garbage: both depict something that started as a product of the human spirit, to reprise Simmel's distinction, and has now been transmuted into something not entirely other, but no longer human either. Images of landfills and ruins present us not just with the spectacle of destruction but also with the spectacle of transformation – a transformation that is not always reassuring. As Stacy Alaimo comments in relation to another inadvertent monument of human civilization, the Great Pacific Garbage Patch, a low-density gyre of plastic debris covering 1.6 million square kilometers, 'ostensibly benign human stuff becomes nightmarish' (Alaimo 2016, 130). This nightmarish dimension, as we will see, is an essential constituent of fictional depictions of ruins.

2.2 The Mushroom and the End of the World

The growing, and perhaps overwhelming, success of the post-apocalyptic genre is intrinsically connected to the diffusion of the imagery of ruins. Contemporary science fiction consistently exploits the scenery of the ruins of the present as a dramatization of the conflicts and anxieties that characterize our age. From the desert London of *The Day of the Triffids* (1951) or *28 Days Later* (2003), which adjourns the London described by Mary Shelley in *The Last Man* (1826), to Will Smith hunting in Central Park in a zombie-ridden New York (*I Am Legend*, 2008), science fiction uses ruins to elicit the emotions of the audience, representing known cities and monuments as derelict and abandoned instead of crowded by masses of tourists. It is no coincidence that ruins appear as a common trope in the imagination of the future: thinking about what lies ahead for humanity means, more often than not, speculating about the possibility of a planet that is more dangerous, and less hospitable, to human life – a planet that is hostile, and from which humanity is progressively expelled. Ruins constitute, again, a symbol of a destructive power that is external to human will and actions, an image of 'a modernity which is now unable to function; ... modernity turned into waste' (Armiero 2021, 14).

As already noted by Burke, there is an inherent sense of spectacle and grandeur in the image of vast monuments turned into ruins as a memento of the passing of time and the perishability of human things. Yet, as we have seen, the true fascination of the ruin, to reprise Georg Simmel, is 'the destruction of the spiritual form by the effect of natural forces, that reversal of the typical order ... felt as a return to the "good mother", as Goethe calls nature' (1958, 382). This reversal is, in itself, neutral – even positive, when we think about projects of urban rewilding. Yet, it is also often seen as negative, truly nightmarish, to reprise Alaimo's wording. Ruins certainly present us with a creative force, but it is a creativity that is not necessarily positive for the human species, as it forces humans to reconsider their position and role in the world.

In the TV series *The Last of Us* (2023), for instance, the 'return to nature' is represented in a negative way, since it involves the action of a parasitic fungus. This reflects a recurrent trope in post-apocalyptic narratives: the relationship between the destroyed landscape and the physical bodies of the survivors. However, this relationship usually involves radiation: mutants are the most common inhabitants of post-apocalyptic wastelands, as a remnant of the perils of degeneration after the fall of civilization. In this vision, humankind becomes a force that turns simultaneously the planet and itself into waste, and the body a place of that encounter with other agencies that characterizes wasting practices. In the case of *The Last of Us*, this is even more significant, as it is not a geological agent that is responsible for the mutations, but a biological agent. As Armiero writes, 'the ruin of modernity does not only reflect onto the dilapidated landscape around the protagonists; it enters their bodies, radically changing the very nature of their being humans' (2021, 14). Centring on a fungus-induced zombie apocalypse, *The Last of Us* follows a traditional pattern of post-disaster narratives: the two protagonists (a man and a teenage girl, Ellie) travel through an American wasteland in search of a cure – the key to which, crucially, might be found in the blood of the girl. As can be expected from a post-apocalyptic series, ruins are a constant presence in the landscapes crossed by the protagonists, and are opposed to the re-purposing of abandoned buildings by the government and other more or less communitarian and autocratic communities. It is no coincidence, we should add, that the series is an adaptation of a video game (with the same title, 2013), as a large number of games, and especially first-person shooters, are actually based around the exploration of abandoned spaces that become sources of peril and danger.

The way in which *The Last of Us* depicts ruins is consistently inspired by the traditional depictions of Romantic and Gothic ruins, with vast sceneries of decay and destruction on a scale that belittles human lives and aspirations. The series tries to convey very explicitly the same feeling of dread associated with the sublime by crafting a series of intericonic references. Towards the half of the first episode, for instance, after two introductory sequences both set in the past (the talk show bit and the first stages of the contagion in Indonesia), viewers are presented with the sight of a ruined Boston being gazed at by a character (seen from behind). This point of view recalls classic Romantic iconography, as in the pose of the *Wanderer above the Sea of Fog* by Caspar David Friedrich (1818). Similarly, in episode 2, we see the protagonists marching towards the city, the ruins of which are seen in the distance, with a composition that recalls, in terms of the proportions of the objects and subjects, Doré's New Zealander in front of the ruins of London – an image that, as we have already mentioned, was directly inspired by Burke's rumination on the destruction of London.

Yet, *The Last of Us* is not simply part of a long genealogy of sublime ruins, but rather derives its power from its representation of uncanny manifestations of non-human agency. Ruination is no longer something that concerns the mineral world and architecture as objects, but rather a dynamic process in which humanity and its artefacts are forced to confront other agencies. *The Last of Us* mobilizes the imagery of plant horror, using botanical elements to convey a sense of dread and the menace of annihilation. Plants, Dawn Keetley argues, 'embody an absolute alterity' (2016, 6); they 'menace with their wild, purposeless growth' (2016, 13), and, most importantly, 'will get their revenge' (2016, 19). Plant horror is not inherently associated with ruins, but it becomes an essential part of the representation of ruins in *The Last of Us*, as the effect of the fungus is that it merges together architectural and physical decay, uniting bodies with spaces, since the super-organism of the fungus colonizes both individuals and spaces (as a character remarks, 'the fungus grows underground. Long fibres like wires, some of them stretching over a mile'). In episode 2, historical buildings are clearly represented as having been colonized by the fungus both in terms of growth on the building, and because they are inhabited by infected people whose bodies have been colonized: the fibrous appendixes of the fungus have grown on the façades of the monuments of Boston in the very same way that they have grown within the bodies of those who have been infected. People have been turned into a small part of the wider fungal ecosystem, just as, in another crucial scene, the infected body of a victim, flourishing with fungal appendixes, is almost fused to a wall. In this sense, the show expresses the dread of non-human agencies whose effects are at play in the process of ruination, and who are getting 'their revenge' against the human species through their purposeless growth and multiplication – purposeless from the perspective of humans, as the scope and aims of the fungus are inscrutable, and therefore much more terrifying. The crucial continuity, in *The Last of Us*, between human bodies and ruins by means of the fungus is important in underlining the way in which ruination involves human beings themselves as a sort of biological 'sacrifice zone', but also the effects of non-human agencies on our species' flesh and spaces alike.

Fungi are not, technically speaking, plants, but the two have long been associated in traditional understandings of the non-human world. Like and indeed even more so than the vegetal, fungi have long been regarded with suspicion by the human species. Their world is, if possible, even more obscure than the vegetal one, and fungi have consistently been seen as agents of decay, dissolution, and death (for a summary of fungiphobia in Western culture, see Rolfe and Rolfe 1974, 54–57). Fungi are seen as a low, unevolved life form, and their proximity causes anxieties related to degeneration and devolution, the threat of 'a degrading return to a less organized primordial state of being', as Anthony Camara writes (2014, 10). In Andrew Moore's photographs of the ruins of Detroit, which are discussed in greater detail in the next section, among the uncanniest are his photographs of books taken over by fungi and moulds, quite literally deformed and merged together into an indistinguishable, 'primordial' mass. In *The Last of Us*, this 'unevolved' form of life is also surprisingly effective in quickly overturning human civilization; the uncanny behaviour of the infected (uncanny because they retain human bodies without adhering to human behaviours, logic, and understanding), their devastated and colonized flesh, and their quirky movements all contribute to a sense of alienness and alterity that is, however, already inherent in the vegetal and fungal world. 'The mushroom at the end of the world', to reprise the title of Anna Tsing's volume on human and non-human entanglements, has become the mushroom responsible for the end of the world: in *The Last of Us*, non-human agencies erode and consume not simply the artefacts of our species but our bodies and minds as well. Tsing writes, in a positive spirit, that 'in a global state of precarity, we don't have choices other than looking for life in this ruin' (2015, 6); the protagonists of the series have to do the very same thing, but they have to do so in order to avoid being killed and colonized by the fungus: searching ruins for traces of a kind of life, specifically the cordyceps, that they need to escape. A frame from *The Last of Us*, extensively used in promoting the series, is especially eloquent in this sense: it is a close-up of an infected human body colonized by the non-human force of the fungus, on the ground and nearly fused with it, transformed to the point of no longer being recognizable as human – and yet it has an unmistakably human eye that carefully watches Ellie's blade. This image powerfully captures not only the interplay between human, non-human, and architectonical elements in the series but also the process of ruination itself, as something that involves a wide variety of agents in a synergy that exceeds human intentionality, and that transforms human spaces and bodies into something else.

2.3 The Fate of the (Human) World

In *The Last of Us*, the non-human world is not entirely reduced to a source of horror, and in the series there are other scenes in which ruins are presented in

Figure 4 Frame of episode 2 of *The Last of Us* (2023), dir. Neil Druckmann.

a less menacing way – in which, in other words, the murderous agency of the non-human is downplayed. A sequence from episode 2, in which the two adults escorting the child are interrogating her about her immunity to the fungus, recalls, in terms of the contrast between lifeless human objects and flourishing non-human life, Moore's famous picture of the internal courtyard of a Detroit school. This scene almost romanticizes decay, with the bright, vivid colours of the plants opposing the greys and beige of the interior of the lifeless building, while Ellie, who is immune to the fungus and thus represents humanity's hope, is immersed in light and vegetation, in contrast to the other characters (see Figure 4). A key influence on the aesthetics of decay of *The Last of Us*, especially in its more neutral forms, was Alan Weisman's bestselling non-fiction book *The World Without Us* (2007), an eloquent example of the use of post-apocalyptic imagination in environmentally themed works (incidentally, another example is Vollmann's *Carbon Ideologies*, which is framed as a letter by the author to humanity in the future, on a poorer, more dangerous, warmer planet). A contemporary classic of environmental non-fiction, Weisman's book is entirely devoted to the narration of human spaces deprived of anthropic life, and the description of the action of non-human entities after human extinction.

The World Without Us is predicated on an essentially sci-fi hypothesis: what would happen if humanity was to suddenly disappear? Weisman adheres to the traditional tropes of the representation of ruins, including presenting readers with magniloquent images of great monuments of humanity turned into ruins. The Statue of Liberty 'ends up at the bottom of the harbor' (2007, 37), an eternal reminder of what humanity was capable of, while the twelfth chapter of the book is explicitly titled 'The Fate of Ancient and Modern Wonders of the World'. This reprises the tendency to ruminate on the devastation of famous monuments – a tendency that, as we have seen, has been consistently exploited in science fiction as well. The Statue of Liberty represented in the closing sequence of *Planet of the Apes* (1968) is one of the first and most famous examples of the use of this specific monument to symbolize the fall of human civilization and the threat of natural elements. The insistence on this particular monument is no coincidence, as the monument is a symbol of New York. The use of New York as a case study for what would happen if humanity disappeared hints at the perceived 'invulnerability' of the city. As Miles Orvell notes, 'just because of its seeming invulnerability and prosperity, New York figures perennially in the cinema of disaster' (2013, 660). New York has, of course, been the target of one of the most intensely mediatized disasters of contemporary history, the 9/11 attacks. Yet, the fact that it has never been the theatre of a war, or bombarded in a formal military action (unlike London, Berlin, or Hiroshima), confers a peculiar sense of invulnerability upon New York. What would happen to New York, Weisman argues, is nothing compared to the September 2001 attack, a 'once-inconceivable calamity' that was, however, 'confined to just a few buildings': on the contrary, 'the time it would take nature to rid itself of what urbanity has wrought may be less than we might suspect' (2007, 21). It is no coincidence, in this sense, that the statue recurs in what is arguably the first Hollywood movie about climate change, Roland Emmerich's *The Day after Tomorrow* (2004). In Emmerich's movie, the Statue of Liberty appears covered in ice as an effect of sudden climate change – an image used in many posters for the movie as well. Here, the statue is not ruined as in *Planet of the Apes*; rather, it is shown at the beginning of a process of ruination, as the city is progressively abandoned: the familiar face of the statue, encrusted in ice, functions as a memento of the power of non-human agencies at play in the Anthropocene, and as a tangible manifestation of the intertwining of human and non-human agencies that occurs in the process of ruination. This is enhanced by the anthropomorphic features of the statue, which make it not only a human-made artefact but also an artefact made in our image.

By depicting the fate of human infrastructures and cultural sites after the disappearance of mankind, Weisman is commenting on the enduring impact of human activities on the planet in ways that resonate with contemporary reflections on the deep chronological timescales of the Anthropocene – timescales that are an essential element of reflections on the sublime. Reflections on long chronologies are a constant: 'after 500 years, what is left depends on where in the world you lived. If the climate was temperate, a forest stands in place of a suburb; minus a few hills, it's begun to resemble what it was before developers, or the farmers they expropriated, first saw it' (2007, 18). Other elements would survive longer, like parts of appliances: 'amid the trees, half-concealed by a spreading understory, lie aluminum dishwasher parts and stainless steel cookware, their plastic handles splitting but still solid' (2007, 18). By explaining how quickly, or not, many human artefacts would disappear, he is highlighting the small scale of human things compared to the rest of the natural world. This double movement is not contradictory: as we have seen earlier, depicting ruins means engaging with the perishability of human things and the vaster temporalities of the non-human world. The deep chronology evoked by traditional ruins, which facilitated a rumination on the passing of time and the inevitable fall of all civilizations, is extended indefinitely in the representations of contemporary ruins, which force viewers to confront vast, inhuman timescales that extend far beyond those of traditional ruins – not for centuries and millennia, but for hundreds of thousands of years. This relativizes the role and importance of the human species on the planet; indeed, as Louise Westling aptly notes, 'the notion of the Anthropocene may itself be an expression of human exceptionalism, when a much broader and deeper look at the Earth's history reveals how late and minimal our impacts have been compared to the enormous dynamism of planetary life' (2022, 1).

Contrary to traditional depictions of ruins, Weisman's portrayal is not peaceful, but rather extremely eventful and crowded – certainly not the 'solitary, deserted sanctuary' celebrated by Diderot, where one 'hear[s] nothing' and is 'isolated from all life's difficulties'. Demonstrating an understanding of ruination as inherently processual, Weisman depicts an urban space that, once human life disappears, is filled with other forms of life: 'while all that disaster was unfolding, squirrels, raccoons, and lizards have been inside, chewing nest holes in the drywall, even as woodpeckers rammed their way through from the other direction' (2007, 17); 'more coyotes follow . . .. Deer, bear, and finally wolves ... arrive in turn. ... Ruins of high-rises echo the love song of frogs breeding in Manhattan's reconstituted streams, now stocked with alewives and mussels dropped by seagulls' (2007, 36–37). Plants, too, penetrate both wood and concrete, quickly and silently demolishing human urban planning: 'as pavement separates, weeds like mustard, shamrock, and goosegrass blow in from Central Park and work their way down the new cracks, which widen further' (2007, 26). Weisman's thought experiment serves to make evident the many agencies intercrossing human ecosystems – agencies that we tend to remove from our conscience but that are present nonetheless. The opening of the book clearly depicts 'nature tak[ing] over', a variety of non-human elements colonizing the spaces from which we attempt to keep them out:

> Even if you live in a denatured, postmodern subdivision where heavy machines mashed the landscape into submission, replacing unruly native flora with

obedient sod and uniform saplings, and paving wetlands in the righteous name of mosquito control – even then, you know that nature wasn't fazed. No matter how hermetically you've sealed your temperature-tuned interior from the weather, invisible spores penetrate anyway, exploding in sudden outbursts of mold – awful when you see it, worse when you don't, because it's hidden behind a painted wall, munching paper sandwiches of gypsum board, rotting studs and floor joists. Or you've been colonized by termites, carpenter ants, roaches, hornets, even small mammals. Most of all, though, you are beset by what in other contexts is the veritable stuff of life: water. It always wants in. (2007, 15–16)

Similar scenery is constantly present in *The Last of Us*, which shows how, over the course of a couple of decades, most human cities and anthropized landscapes have been reabsorbed by natural elements. Yet, while Weisman is technically describing an apocalyptic event (the disappearance of the human species, as would be the case in the event of a nuclear holocaust), what he is truly addressing is a process that is already occurring, one that human societies simply try to keep at bay, and it is no coincidence that, later in the book, he uses the abandoned town of Varosha, in the buffer zone between north and south Cyprus, as an example of what will happen to the planet. Varosha, in this sense, is a space in which Weisman's 'apocalypse' has already happened, though what has happened there is not the result of an apocalypse at all, but rather a process that is already taking place outside our perception: 'if you're a homeowner, you already knew it was only a matter of time for yours, but you've resisted admitting it, even as erosion callously attacked, starting with your savings. Back when they told you what your house would cost, nobody mentioned what you'd also be paying so that nature wouldn't repossess it long before the bank' (2007, 16). Indeed, it is just human care and activity that prevent these creations from turning into ruins, as if ruination and decay were processes constantly ongoing in the world and could only be partially and momentarily stopped.

It is no coincidence that ruins are a commonplace in post-apocalyptic imagery, because, given that 'apocalypse' means literally 'revelation', ruins are nothing but spaces revealed to be what they always truly were, spaces in which processes that were already ongoing manifest themselves to the unwilling members of the human species that try to prevent them. It is precisely in this sense that a discussion of ruins necessitates the adoption of a negative ecology, meaning an ecology of the margins, which highlights that the derelict and abandoned spaces are really flourishing and ripe with potentiality and life. This understanding can be positive or negative, evoke relief or fear, and be a source of amusement or understanding. We have explored both of these responses in this section; in the next section, we will see how the negative perception of ruins is dramatized in contemporary culture.

3 An Ecology of Negativity

3.1 A Gothic Anthropocene

We have noted that, in *The Last of Us*, the ruined buildings of post-disaster America are modelled on traditional depictions of sublime ruins; however, another model is active beneath this surface – Detroit. The ruined and crumbled urban spaces that the protagonists cross throughout the series are those of great American industrial metropolises whose growth has been suddenly halted, whose population has been reduced, and whose buildings have been mostly abandoned or destroyed. Once again, this is not just sci-fi speculation, but rather something that has already, albeit partially, happened to the city of Detroit, a former industrial capital of the world that was plunged, in the second half of the twentieth century, into a deep economic, social, and environmental crisis. A privileged subject in contemporary representations of ruins, Detroit is a city whose progressive urban decay, due to a combination of infrastructural collapse and de-industrialization, has become the epitome of mournful ruminations on the decline of the American empire. This section discusses Detroit as a paradigm of the ruins of modernity, and thus as a reflection of the (un) sustainability of industrial society. It also addresses the issue of environmental justice in relation to ruins, pointing out how the distinction between those who are left inhabiting a ruined landscape and those who can afford to abandon it reflects existing racial and class inequalities.

As a case study, Detroit has been extensively discussed in several books and papers, as well as in the national and international press; this focus on Detroit has also been heavily criticized by locals as a romanticization of decay that has little to say about the actual lives of the city's inhabitants and the socio-economic conditions that led to the ruination of the metropolis. This section is less interested in Detroit as a city than as a figure of the imagination. Detroit's ruins have been metabolized in our imagery to such an extent that they have functioned as the backdrop for horror movies like *Only Lovers Left Alive* (2013), *It Follows* (2014), *Don't Breathe* (2016), and *Barbarian* (2022), which repurpose the Gothic component of ruins – with the crucial difference that, in these movies, vampires and monsters do not find refuge among the derelict remnants of a long-gone world, but in everyday houses and buildings, such as can be found in most American towns. This spectral take on a post-industrial environment is also reflected in the work of photographers Andrew Moore, Yves Marchand, and Romain Meffre, whose depictions of ruined areas of Detroit reflect and adjourn Romantic and Gothic aesthetics.

The word 'Gothic' has been evoked several times in this Element: ruins are one of the constituents of Gothic imagery, with crumbled castles and the solitary remnants of old buildings functioning as the setting for the misadventures of the protagonists. Yet, when discussing *The Last of Us*, but also Vollmann, we have already mobilized the critical lexicon of the Gothic: one of spectral hauntings and dreadful returns. The Gothic has been extensively defined as the form of the return of the removed and the repressed; its imagery is crowded with manifestations of things that are believed to have passed and yet refuse to do so, things societies have removed from public life and from the space of the speakable that yet return to haunt them. This is not only the case with ghosts and the undead, but also, clearly, with ruins; as a tangible manifestation of a past that still lives in the present, ruins have been a common trope in many Gothic texts.

The Gothic has been described as a negative aesthetic, meaning an aesthetic that, historically, defines itself in opposition to the rationality of the Enlightenment, and in which what is traditionally considered negative acquires a renewed importance and value: 'Gothic', David Punter writes, 'was the archaic, the pagan, that which was prior to, or was opposed to, or resisted the establishment of civilised values and a well-regulated society' (1980, 3). This is also true in an ecological sense, and especially in relation to ruins, whose aesthetic value derives from the intervention of non-human elements that contradict the organizing principles of our civilization. We have seen the extent to which, in ruins, things and agencies that are not supposed to manifest themselves, that our societies and cultures banish to the margins, come back. In this sense, in describing the ruins of West Virginia and Fukushima or the fungal ecosystem of *The Last of Us*, we are participating in an ecogothic approach – an approach that highlights 'the fear, anxiety, and dread' not just of the past and its uncanny return but also of the relationships between human and non-human worlds (Keetley and Sivils 2017, 1).

As mentioned, reflecting on ruins necessitates adopting a negative ecology, but also envisioning an ecology of negativity, in which things that hold a negative value in our system of thought find a new meaning and function, in ways that counter anthropocentric views. In the plant horror of *The Last of Us*, in the representation of the fungus-dominated world, we can point to what we could call an 'ecophobic response', to reprise the terminology coined by Simon C. Estok. As the word clearly suggests, ecophobia is a fear of nature, which, of course, implies 'an antagonism between humans and their environments' that can 'embody fear, contempt, indifference, or lack of mindfulness (or some combination of these) toward the natural environment' (1). Crucially, 'ecophobia is all about frustrated agency' (10), meaning that the sentiment of ecophobia is simultaneously a fear of the agency of nature, and a reaction to something that limits human agency. Ruins embody an ecophobic view insofar as they represent the apparently purposelessness victory of 'nature' over 'spirit', while simultaneously substituting human agency with several contradicting and yet coexisting non-human agencies.

Of course, the Gothic also encapsulates the Anthropocene itself, an age of catastrophes and disasters, in which the agencies of the natural world, long presumed to have been controlled and contained, manifest themselves in opposition to humanity. Justin D. Edwards, Rune Graulund, and Johan Höglund have described the Anthropocene in these terms, noting how 'Nature in the Anthropocene is rapidly drifting beyond our control in ways that are far more complex – yet at the same time also frighteningly literal – than ever before' (Edwards, Graulund, and Höglund 2022, xiv). The imaginative tools of the Gothic have the potential to represent the constant transgression of nature–culture boundaries that characterizes the Anthropocene (2022, ix) and that is one of the constituents of the imagery of ruins and the contemporary sublime. The Gothic's fascination with excess and negativity 'makes it a supremely suitable chronicler of the violence of climate change and of the human being's tentacular connection to all uncanny, damaged life on this planet'; life in the Anthropocene means 'to recognize that transgression, excess, and monstrosity are no longer anomalies in human life but inextricable parts of it' (2022, xi–xii).

Contemporary scholars across the environmental humanities have increasingly employed the lexicon of the Gothic to discuss the current environmental situation (the Gothic-ness of the Anthropocene), but also to discuss the relationships and entanglements at play within ecosystems. As Anne Tsing et al. write, 'every landscape is haunted by past ways of life' (2017, 2), both human and non-human, by extinction and changes in balance. We have discussed Vollmann's reportages as depicting haunted landscapes: spaces of destruction where we also bear witness to the uncanny survival of agencies (radioactivity, chemicals) that are dangerous to human life – such agencies are uncanny because they are invisible and ubiquitous, like a supernatural force or a ghost. 'Haunting' is an inherently Gothic word, of course, one that refers to the uneasy survival of the past into the present. This is particularly true in the case of Detroit, a cityscape that, in being haunted by the ruins of its industrial past, is also haunted by those of the futures that such ruins, in their time, promised.

That Detroit's ruins have a Gothic component is pretty evident – not least because most of the ruined buildings in question were built in a Neo-gothic or Victorian style, as in the case of the United Artists Theater. However, Detroit Gothic is a particular kind of Gothic, characterized not by the survival of the antique, but rather by the present – and not any kind of present, not a present shaped by accidental abandonment or natural disaster, but a post-industrial present. The industrial ruins of Detroit certainly hint at decay and the perishability of things, as all ruins do, but they are also more markedly ecological in the way in which they highlight the unsustainability of a form of economic development and the persistence of non-human agencies. At the same time,

Detroit's ruins 'reflect and draw attention to invisibility or failures of vision and, relatedly, to the sense of risk that many see as a characteristic feature of modern society' (Wagner 2020, 67), while also showcasing the possibilities of ruins.

3.2 'My parents wouldn't allow me to go south of 8 Mile'

Gothic imagery is so associated with Detroit that the latter has become a feature of political discourse in the United States, and not just at a local level; it is viewed as the very epitome of American decline at an international level. During his 2016 presidential inauguration, Trump explicitly evoked the funereal and macabre lexicon of the Gothic romance to describe the disarrayed American provinces he so eagerly wanted to make 'great again' (eight years later, on the eve of the 2024 presidential election, while rallying for Trump, billionaire Elon Musk proclaimed himself 'dark, Gothic MAGA', which stands for 'Make America Great Again', but that at this point could equally be read as 'Make America Gothic Again'):

> Mothers and children trapped in poverty in our inner cities, rusted-out factories, scattered like tombstones across the landscape of our nation, an education system flush with cash, but which leaves our young and beautiful students deprived of all knowledge, and the crime, and the gangs, and the drugs that have stolen too many lives and robbed our country of so much unrealized potential. This American carnage stops right here and stops right now. (Trump 2017)

Rusted-out factories as tombstones for the American dream are, again, a commonplace in fictional and documentary depictions of Detroit. Interestingly, the same imagery recurs even in anti-Trump Republican opposition, as in the case of 'Mourning in America', a one-minute commercial describing the shortfalls of Trump's presidency and opposing his 2020 re-election campaign.[5] The video heavily features the ruins of Detroit (as well as images of Covid-19 patients, as if to strengthen the feeling of impending doom they convey) as a symbol of a decaying country. 'Mourning in America' is a pun on Ronald Reagan's 'Morning in America' (Wood 2021, 51–52), but it is also, clearly, another word associated with death and funerals, abandonment and decay – a word that might be more appropriate in graveyard poetry than political discourse. In the words of Andrew Wood, 'Trump's image of factories, corroded and in disrepair, littering the national landscape, serves as both memorial and monument to a moribund economy' (Wood 2021, 64).

It could hardly be denied that, despite recent encouraging signs of a resurgence, Detroit is a city in crisis. Once the world's capital of car

---

[5] www.youtube.com/watch?v=t_yG_-K2MDo.

production (an industry that comprised the majority of the city's economy), following a crisis in the automobile sector in the 1970s and a mix of delocalization and relocation, Detroit's population plummeted, and social and racial tensions became increasingly harsh. Crucially, the urban development of the city in its growing years was informed by a de facto segregationist model, with the vast and impoverished African-American population forced to live in cheap homes in the city, and the white middle class located in the more affluent suburbs (it should be noted, incidentally, that the Industrial Revolution itself and the subsequent social and environmental processes have been extensively read in Gothic terms; see Marshall 2021). Today, 'what is now the poorest city in the nation, which is overwhelmingly black, is also bordered on the north by some of the wealthiest suburbs in the nation, which are overwhelmingly white' (Apel 2015, 4). The shrinking of the automobile industry and therefore of the local government has left many communities in disarray, due to unemployment as well as infrastructural collapse – and private and public misfortunes have caused the abandonment of buildings that has resulted in Detroit's famous ruins (indeed, 'one doesn't have to travel to Iraq to contemplate today's relationship between capitalism and ruin'; Stoler 2013, 115).

In recent years, Detroit has held the record for the highest murder rate in the country per capita (40.7 homicides per 100,000 residents in 2008, with 1,220 violent crimes per 100,000 residents), while governmental agencies and infrastructures have been progressively reduced (including, for instance, firefighters: in 2008, Detroit reported 90,000 fires, while twice the amount occurred in New York, despite the latter being more than ten times more populous). Population also declined, going from two million in the twentieth century to slightly less than 700,000, with the result that there is an extraordinary number of abandoned buildings – around 90,000 (all data taken from Binelli 2012, 9). About 40 per cent of streetlights do not work, the unemployment rate is a remarkable 23 per cent, and 40 per cent of Detroitians live below the poverty line (Apel 2015, 4).

Of course, such a grim portrait does not exhaust the reality of Detroit; 'the Motor City is more than a grid of vacant lots and broken tooth neighborhoods. There is also plenty of start-up spirit, a new confidence working to reconfigure Detroit into a center of U.S. post-industrialization', with volunteers taking care of disarranged neighbours and enterpreneurs and artists moving to take 'advantage of dirt-cheap housing and a hunger for new ideas' (Wood 2021, 94). Yet, in the public perception, Detroit is not these things, but rather a space of ruin. Indeed, Detroit embodies 'two cities – the real one with all its complexities and histories, and the one fashioned through ruin images' (Apel 2015, 4). As Ann Laura Stoler comments, 'in mythological terms . . . Detroit remains the ancestral birthplace of storied American capitalism' (2013, 117), and its downfall is akin to the fall of an empire – as indeed the automobile industry of Detroit shaped American dominion throughout the twentieth century (Charlie Erwin Wilson, CEO of General Motors and later Secretary of Defence under Dwight Eisenhower, famously said that 'what was good for [America] was good for General Motors, and vice versa'; in Stoler 2013, 117).

Yet, the fall of the American empire epitomized by Detroit is not the consequence of an invasion or a military defeat; rather, it is the result of an increasingly dematerialized, ghostly economy, and an unequal distribution of resources. In a globalized, neoliberal economic system there is no contradiction between the accumulation of unprecedented levels of wealth in the United States (the markets flourishing with investors and speculation), and the crumbling of the symbols of their rise to planetary domination. As Stoler notes, 'in Rome, the ruins came after the empire fell. In the United States, the destruction of Detroit happened even as the country was rising to new heights as a superpower' (2013, 126). While immaterial wealth migrates and detaches itself from its locality, those who are left behind have to endure the disarray and abandonment; they have, in other words, to live among the ruins of a decentralized and globalized economy. Detroit is not a post-apocalyptic wasteland of the kind envisioned by Weisman, a post-disaster landscape like Fukushima; it is, rather, a 'postindustrial wasteland' (Kinney 2016, xi).

As happened in the late eighteenth century with Volney, Detroit's ruins have become a pillar of political discourse. Yet, it is a kind of discourse that omits the wasting relationship at the core of Detroit's ruination, the profound racial inequality and environmental injustice regulating its creation and demise, with the vast African-American population left behind by the government and investors alike. While Trump's discourse appears to identify one key feature of environmental justice (the ruined, unsanitary spaces of deindustrialization, which are 'like tombstones'), it does not fully comprehend it, as it ignores all the actual demographics and identities of the individuals involved in this relationship. The mothers and children he evokes 'are not marked with particular identities. Their lack of demographic peculiarities allow all audience members to place themselves amongst the ruins, to project themselves against that decline, and to see themselves as co-producers of a new age' (Wood 2021, 66).

In keeping with its Gothic status, as mentioned, Detroit has, in recent years, also served as the setting for several horror movies in which the ruined cityscape is not simply used as the backdrop for stories of terror and the supernatural, but also becomes an essential constituent of them, an integral part of that return of the repressed that takes place in these movies. Among these movies, *It Follows* is especially relevant not only in its depiction of ruins but also in the way it addresses the subtle racial and social inequalities at play in the urban environment. The movie is centred around a mysterious curse, which transmits itself through sexual contact. After having intercourse with Hugh, Jay, the protagonist, is threatened by a supernatural entity (the 'It' of the title) that takes the form of many different people, some familiar and some unknown to her; if the entity reaches her, it will kill her, and the only way to get rid of it is to have sex with someone else and pass the curse along, as Hugh did with her. Should the entity kill her, it would then start hunting Hugh again, and then the person who passed it to him, and so on. Jay, helped by her sister and a group of friends and neighbours, tries to fight the entity, first seeking refuge outside the city, then passing it to a willing neighbour who doubts the truthfulness of the curse, and finally ambushing it and electrocuting it in the swimming pool. All of these attempts, however, fail, and at the end of the movie Jay has sex with Paul, a childhood friend, having agreed that he would then pass it on to a sex worker. Yet, it is not clear whether this actually happens (we see Paul driving near some sex workers in his car, but not approaching them), and in the last scene of the movie Jay and Paul are depicted walking together hand in hand, with a figure behind them in the distance that may, or may not, be the entity.

The movie is a variation on the classic slasher formula, according to which teenage characters tend to die sooner the more sexually active they are; and it has been read as a reflection on the ethics and constrictions of heteronormative monogamy (Church 2021, 181–212). Yet, given the scope of this Element, it is the setting of *It Follows* that is of most interest, including the role of ruins in its imagery and the depiction of the relationship between the inner city and the suburbs as involving an inherent process of othering, which, as we have seen, is central to contemporary discussions of waste and ruination. In *It Follows*, the traditional haunted house or castle of the Gothic novel and the horror movie disappear, only to be substituted by everyday and industrial spaces in ruins. From a genre perspective, the truly genial trait of *It Follows* lies in the nature of the entity, which can take the form of any individual, thereby forcing the characters to be on the lookout for it constantly, unsure whether they are seeing regular people or the entity. The viewer has to do the same thing, frantically searching the frame for 'it' to appear. The indecipherability of the entity means that any space can potentially become a place of haunting: it transforms any corner of Detroit into a Gothic space, and implies that, much more than individual relationships or psychological dynamics, the movie 'casts the environmental, infrastructural, and material stratification of society as the primary source of dread' (Kelly 2017, 3).

Some of the crucial scenes of the movie take place among ruins, from Jay's first encounter with 'it' to her search for information in an abandoned house.

Even when they are not in ruins, the internal settings and various details suggest a somehow derelict condition through the merging of elements from the past: the soundtrack hints at 1980s music, the furniture recalls the 1970s, and the protagonists watch old black-and-white movies on television (Church 2021, 183). Despite not being explicitly set in the past, the movie lacks elements that clearly point to its being set in the present: Jay, for instance, does not look for information about her curse on the internet, as it is customary in horror films of this kind. This, consequently, gives viewers the impression that the movie is set in a time outside of time, conveying a certain stillness that is coherent with the trope of ruins, as if Detroit had been abandoned by history and could survive only with remnants of things that have gone before.

As the title suggests, *It Follows* is a movie that is profoundly concerned with mobility. The fact that the entity 'follows', that it is mobile, hints at the placelessness of global capitalism, and at the de-localization that rendered Detroit what it is now. But of course it is the city of Detroit itself that is concerned with mobility, being the birthplace of the American automobile industry. Cars are a vital part of the movie: Jay 'acquires the curse during sex in the back of Hugh/Jeff's 1975 Plymouth Gran Fury' (Church 2021, 199), a vehicle manufactured in Detroit that also appears on the movie posters. The scene is shot outside Northville Psychiatric Hospital (see Figure 5), while the following scene (in which Hugh ties her to a wheelchair to explain the nature of the curse to her) is set inside the empty Packard Automotive Plant, one of the symbols of Detroit's de-industrialization (Taylor 2020, 159; see Figure 6). The ability to move around is essential to the possibility of escaping the curse, and this movement needs to be made by automobile.

It Follows is a movie about precarity in which young people appear to be entirely left on their own (adults seldom appear in the movie, and Jay is brought up by a single mother – her father being one of the forms the entity takes), and are

Figure 5 Frame from *It Follows* (2014), dir. David Robert Mitchell.

Figure 6 Frame from *It Follows* (2014), dir. David Robert Mitchell.

forced to navigate the vast ruinscape of Detroit and to confront the processes of othering and segregation active in it. The movie starts in a more or less peaceful suburb of Detroit, but, in her attempts to escape the entity, the protagonist has to cross other, less prosperous areas, visit ruined buildings, and finally enter the inner city. This movement is explicitly thematized in the movie, with one character saying: 'When I was a little girl my parents would't allow me to go south of 8 Mile and I didn't even know what that meant until I got a little older and I started realizing that's where the city started and the suburbs ended.' 8 Mile is the road in Detroit that separates the suburbs from the more degraded inner city, the white community and the African-American community. Thus, it is significant that the movie features almost no black people – one of the few black characters is perhaps an incarnation of the entity and is therefore associated with dread and menace. That the white, middle-class kids from the suburbs encounter almost no African-Americans, and when they do they fear them, is reflective of the oblique way in which the movie addresses the racial question at the core of Detroit's ruination.

In *It Follows*, moving across Detroit involves facing increasingly dangerous situations the closer the protagonist and her friends get to the centre of the city, to its ruined and abandoned spaces. In this sense, Detroit is 'establish[ed] ... as a monstrous place accustomed to neglect and violence; a place to kill and a place to die' (Taylor 2020, 160); 'the closer to the inner city the older and more antiquated the infrastructure, the more modest the housing, the more ominous the living conditions' (Kelly 2017, 9). Unlike the photographic depictions of Detroit we are about to discuss, *It Follows* is not a movie concerned with ecophobia or the returned of the environmentally repressed. It is, however, a movie in which the Gothic narrative tool of the curse allows the re-emergence of a relationship of othering and waste that is encapsulated in the ruined cityscape.

3.3 Mourning (or Not) in America

Like Chernobyl and Fukushima, Detroit too has become a site of 'dark tourism': there are numerous, popular organized tours of Detroit's ruins (Whitehouse 2018, 4), not unlike those one can undertake in Pompeii and Herculaneum. This ambivalent fascination is also the result of a consistent aestheticization, in recent years, of Detroit's ruins, which have piqued the curiosity of several photographers, from the early explorations of Camilo José Vergara (*American Ruins*, 1999) to Yves Marchand and Romain Meffre's *The Ruins of Detroit* (2010), Andrew Moore's *Detroit Disassembled* (2010), and Dan Austin and Sean Doerr's *Lost Detroit* (2010). The works of these photographers vary: if Vergara, for instance, seems to be more interested in documenting a sociological condition, Marchand and Meffre, as well as Moore, turn Detroit into a site of wonder and dread that is inherently Gothic – even if their portrayals are not identical.

Clearly, such aestheticized depictions of Detroit's ruins risk falling under the label of 'ruin porn', which we have already discussed – and it is important to note that the term 'ruin porn' appears to have been coined specifically in reference to Detroit by James Griffioen, a Detroit resident interviewed by the indie online magazine *Vice* (Whitehouse 2018, 54; on the concept of ruin porn, see Pétursdóttir and Olsen 2014a, and the responses to their article included in the same issue; and Lyons 2018). As mentioned, the idea of a pornography of ruins refers to a tendency to represent ruins without taking into account their historical and cultural significance, experiencing them instead as cheap thrills, easy sources of interest or pleasure without reflecting on the complexity of the stories and lives behind, and among, them (Wood 2021, 102–3). The label of 'ruin porn' is not theoretical, of course, but rather situated, as it 'depends on a dichotomy between insiders and outsiders, between those who regard themselves as city loyalists whose lives and work are affected by the city and have therefore earned the right to profit from it and those whose photos they regard as voyeuristic and exploitative, feeding off the city's misery while understanding little about its problems, histories, or dreams' (Apel 2015, 23). However, this is not a dichotomy without victims: being the subject of ruin porn, or living in a city that is its subject, might mean 'internaliz[ing] an image of the city as a site of failure, . . .a source of demoralization and embarrassment' (Apel 2015, 23).

In the case of Detroit, this is particularly relevant. The photographs of Moore and of Marchand and Meffre portray the ruins of the city as abstract spaces, deprived of human life, but seldom take into account the processes of othering and exploitation associated with the ruins, especially as they affect the African-American community. The few depictions of people we find in those books, mostly depictions of people of African-American descent, feel exploitative (Somhegyi 2020, 122): photographs taken from afar, without any true interaction with the subjects, members of Detroit's black community, as if they were but props in the ruined landscapes, like the shepherds in eighteenth-century ruin paintings.

Yet, despite their abstract tone, the works of Moore and of Marchand and Meffre offer a powerful, and positively Gothic, view of the ruins of Detroit. They try to elicit a sense of the sublime by showing the destruction of human monuments by natural elements, and the spectral vestiges of such monuments after their abandonment. Marchand and Meffre, who 'aim to put the works in a larger aesthetic-historical framework' (Somhegyi 2020, 120), make a direct comparison between the *Ruinenlust* of old and what has happened to Detroit in more recent years. As they write on their website:

> Detroit, industrial capital of the XXth Century, played a fundamental role shaping the modern world. The logic that created the city also destroyed it. Nowadays, unlike anywhere else, the city's ruins are not isolated details in the urban environment. They have become a natural component of the landscape. Detroit presents all archetypal buildings of an American city in a state of mummification. Its splendid decaying monuments are, no less than the Pyramids of Egypt, the Coliseum of Rome, or the Acropolis in Athens, remnants of the passing of a great Empire.[6]

The photographers' wording creates a clear link between their work and traditional theorizations of ruins: Detroit is seen as the ideal continuation of the ruined scenery of ancient Rome and Greece. In the text accompanying their photographs, they are even more explicit, describing the ruins of Detroit as 'the volatile result of a change of era and the fall of empires' (the reference to empires being, of course, another suggestion of antiquity), and a 'natural and sublime demonstration of our human destinies and of their paradoxes, a dramatization of our creative and self-destructive vanities' (2010, 16).

In keeping with this understanding of the ruins of Detroit, the photographs of Marchand and Meffre highlight the vast, inhuman aspects of the buildings they depict. The roof of the Packard Automotive Plant – collapsed and sunken as if due to the actions of a giant – and the ample, empty industrial halls of the Global American Steel Company suggest an old grandeur that is now incompatible with human life, too great and distant from everyday humanity (as Apel notes, in the 230 pages of Marchand and Meffre's book, only two images include human subjects and one of these images depicts the photographers themselves, 2015, 79–85; there are even fewer in Moore). The cover of their book is eloquent in this

---

[6] www.marchandmeffre.com/detroit.

Figure 7 *Michigan Central Station, Detroit*, 2007, by Yves Marchand & Romain Meffre. Courtesy of the authors.

sense (see Figure 7): Michigan Central Station, one of the most iconic symbols of Detroit's ruination, is framed in order 'to allow no space outside the cool gray tones of the structure itself so that we are drawn through the broken windows toward the interior darkness' (Apel 2015, 79–85). The claustrophobic atmosphere of the picture is suggestive, and emphasizes the monumental allure of the building in ways that are reminiscent of the exaggerated proportions of Piranesi's Roman ruins (it helps that the station itself was partially modelled on classic architecture). The station is also, of course, another symbol of the city's infrastructural collapse, an example not only of its architectural glory but also of an age of movement and connection that is now past.

Marchard and Meffre do, however, depict human remnants and traces of their presence – and they do so in quite a macabre manner. A series of images of Highland Park Police Station immortalize forensic evidence left behind after the closure of the station, including elements from the case of serial killer Benjamin Atkins, who, as the photographers note, raped and killed eleven women between 1991 and 1992. Atkins targeted mostly sex workers and drug addicts, and left their bodies in abandoned spaces and ruined buildings. By photographing the forensic material in the ruined scenery of the abandoned police station,

Marchand and Meffre are doing many things at once: commenting on the collapse of the governmental infrastructures of Detroit; depicting the transformation of human biological remains into part of the ruined scenery; and also exploiting for aesthetic purposes a case of violent crime that speaks to the economic and racial inequalities of Detroit without actually addressing these inequalities. The spectacularization of such gruesome details directly refers to the imagery of horror (serial killers like Atkins are a popular subject in horror cinema): in Austin and Doerr's *Lost Detroit*, we find a picture of the interior of Broderick Tower – the eerie light of the sunset obliquely illuminates graffiti of the number 666, famously associated with Satanism. The effect is that of a space transfigured into a menacing version of its former self.

Moore, too, has captured the decayed scenery of Detroit in ways that closely recall traditional depictions of ruins evoking the sublime, but in a different way to Marchand and Meffre: he is less interested in the grandeur of ruins and more interested in the non-human agencies at play in ruins. As Miles Orvell notes, Moore is 'a photographer working within the discourse of the poetic sublime, which represents the ruin as a symbol of time and nature's revenge upon human exertion', for whom Detroit is 'a perfect space for a meditation on the melancholy passage of time' (Orvell 2013, 653). While it has many points in common with Marchand and Meffre's work (several photographs in the two books immortalize the same places, even the same details), Moore's work is less focused on the monumental aspect of Detroit and more concerned with the processual nature of ruination, with Detroit as a space in which non-human agencies re-emerge. As Moore explicitly states in the text accompanying the photographs,

> Detroit's transfiguration has led it beyond decay into a surreal landscape, where the past is receding so quickly that time itself seems to be distorted.... What was once America's fourth largest city, spread across 138 square miles, is now one-third empty land. Many of these empty stretches are now fields of high grass. If the roads were overgrown, some neighbourhoods would resemble prairies. Formerly manicured courtyards have become impassable forests, trees sprout from cornices of office buildings, and former living rooms lie suspended in the rising underground. (2010, 119)

The depiction of nature taking over human spaces aims to elicit, according to Moore himself, a 'romantic sense of horror and beauty' (in Apel 2015, 85–90), and is in line with contemporary representations of ruins in its attention to the action of non-human agencies. A renowned work like *Birches Growing in Rotting Books, Detroit* (2008), already mentioned in relation to *The Last of Us*, is especially eloquent in this sense.[7] Depicting young trees growing inside an

---

[7] The picture can be seen here: https://andrewlmoore.com/detroit.

abandoned Detroit school, with mouldering books scattered on the floor, the picture encapsulates the intrinsic contradiction of the ruin as something that illustrates the effects of natural elements on cultural artefacts. The fact that the building depicted here is a school (a communal space and a site of learning), and the floor is covered with books, offers an especially compelling synthesis of these two elements: natural agents crawl back into a space that is now bereft of human lives, in which the symbols of human culture appear to be devoured by decay, progressively putrefied, 'encrusted with some unidentifiable organic coating that looks like the growth of a coral reef' (Orvell 2013, 654). Yet, in opposition to the decaying Gothic interior of the school, the courtyard in which the trees are growing represents an image of openness, from which the light of the picture emanates. The camera angle is simultaneously intimate and claustrophobic, as the vantage point is inside the building: the angular perspective makes the patios of the abandoned school look vaster and more cavernous, as in a contemporary rendition of J. M. W. Turner's *The Crypt of Kirkstall Abbey* (1812), in which the light obliquely penetrates the vaults of the crypt, illuminating not vegetation but a group of resting cows (Piccini 2014, 31). This stylistic choice enhances the ambiguity of the portrayal, as destructive natural forces seem to be portrayed in a positive, hopeful light.

While Moore occasionally plays on the sense of grandeur that is already inherent in the grand buildings of Detroit, be they public spaces like Michigan Central Station or factories like the River Rouge Complex, what differentiates Moore's work from that of his Romantic precursors is the fact that, for the most part, he is not portraying known monuments but everyday spaces. As noted by Dora Apel, if the classical ruin was the result of a finished process, contemporary ruins are ongoing, in formation; they are not a surviving, albeit mutilated, symbol of an ancient past, but rather a symbol of our own present turning inevitably into a past (Apel 2015, 12–13). In this sense, then, the 'forces which give a mountain its shape', to reprise Simmel, are shown at work not just on the grand remnants of the cities of old but also on the spaces and objects with which we interact every day. These feelings of inherent precariousness are important from an ecological perspective, as they remind viewers of the processes of environmental decay occurring at a planetary level, and the vital part non-human agencies play in all human ecosystems.

The spaces photographed by Moore are transformed by the non-human agencies that set in after the departure of humans. Moore captures the ponds and the small stalactites that have formed in the abandoned factories, which have turned into semi-natural landscapes no longer fit for human life. In other pictures, like that of a former paintball arena, consumer goods have become an undifferentiated carpet of trash, with small patches of green flourishing in empty areas. This is consistent throughout Moore's work, whose most impressive frames are devoted to the intersection of natural elements and formerly human spaces. Moore often immortalizes decaying books, countless pages of paper devoured by mould and fungi and reshaped into something barely recognizable, an amorphous mass; in a close-up of such a mass, it is not even clear that we are inside a building, and if it were not for a couple of more or less intact books in the upper part of the picture, it could easily be mistaken for a landscape photograph depicting canyons from a distance. In other shots, he simply documents the crawling vegetation within buildings, as in the case of the grass that now carpets the floors of the Ford Motor Company former headquarters, while, in his depictions of houses, Moore privileges those that have been completely devoured by vegetation, such that they are just in the shape of a house, with no architectonical elements visible.

One image that is especially powerful, by virtue of its simplicity, is the photograph of Arnold Nursing Home. As in Friedrich's Oybin monastery, in this image, too, the window frames a patch of the garden outside, again creating a stark contrast between the lifelessness of the interior, which contains a few broken pieces of furniture, and the vitality and light of the outside; and we, as viewers, are invited to re-think the natural elements we are seeing in light of their interaction with the ruined surroundings. If, to reprise Friedrich's title, we are to identify with the dreamer, then this dream is much less peaceful than that of the Romantics, and even has a nightmarish quality: on the wall on the right, a piece of graffiti sinisterly reads, 'God has left Detroit'. Ruins, as we have seen, are the product of an absence that is then filled; therefore, it might be the case that God has left Detroit only for something else to take his place.

4 The Promises of Ghosts

4.1 Anthropocene Nostalgia

Among the ruins of Detroit, one image appears to be especially striking and haunting, as testified by the fact that it recurs in both Moore's work and Marchand and Meffre's work. It is a picture of a clock hanging on the wall of the Cass Technical High School building: its face has melted in a Dalí-esque manner, turning it into a concrete image of the subversion of human time that occurs in the process of ruination.[8] We have seen how decay has transformed Detroit into a surreal landscape, where the remnants of the past can be found side by side with previously banished forms of life and new social and cultural practices. In the depictions of Detroit's ruins, time appears distorted and

---

[8] The picture can be seen here: https://andrewlmoore.com/detroit.

collapsed, quite literally (if we look at the clock's hands) out of joint, to reprise Jacques Derrida's hauntological discussion of *Hamlet* (1993). Such collapse, however, is intrinsic to ruination, inasmuch as it creates a space that forces us to confront non-human chronologies and put our knowledge and understanding of human artefacts into perspective. As Aleksandra Prica notes, 'ruins manifest a specific textuality that productively unsettles chronologies, histories, and meaning making as we have come to know them' (2022, 6). Prica points to the role of decay in ruins as underlining their processual nature, which is to say that it invites us to understand ruins not as 'static entities but subject to change – usually as a result of slow, fast, or even sudden disintegration' (7). The slowness of the process of ruination contributes to this chronological unsettling, as it takes place on scales with which humans are unfamiliar.

We have already mentioned ruins' complex chronology: namely, the fact that they involve temporal spans that are vastly larger than those of human lives and civilizations – inhuman chronologies that resonate with the temporal shift imposed by the Anthropocene. This section takes into account another aspect of this issue: ruins' relationship with nostalgia. Ruins are traditionally associated with nostalgia, both politically and environmentally, but to what extent is nostalgia useful in addressing contemporary ecological concerns? In some environmentalist rhetoric, ruins become a space of openness, rewilding, and coexistence: once the human species has retreated, nature can flourish in the abandoned spaces left behind. Other discussions of ruins insist on their being remnants of a past of greatness, making them a symbol of regressive nostalgia. Specifically, this section discusses what Jacob C. Miller calls the 'retail ruin' (2023) as both a symbol of the caducity of capitalist culture, and a re-semantization of the non-places of capitalism into spaces that are inherently imbued with history, thereby addressing ruins' capacity to signify many things and intersect many temporal planes at once, while simultaneously opening up and precluding new environmental futures.

Nostalgia is one of the constituent elements of today's cultural milieu. It is a commonplace, in discourses about contemporary media, to point out that we live in an age of reunions, remakes, and reboots, as if the only way of ensuring the success of a product is to give audiences a new iteration of a formerly successful one. Nostalgia is also crucial in contemporary politics, especially in the regressive tendencies of populism. In the slogan 'Make America Great Again', the crucial word is not 'great', but rather 'again': it is not greatness (a rather vague concept) per se that is valued, but the act of returning. This is a return to an idealized past, a mythic vision of an America that never really was but that still exerts its power on the present. In one of his latest essays, Zygmunt Bauman has clearly defined the tendency of the present to escape an uncertain future through a movement towards a secure past: 'The road to future', he writes, 'turns looks uncannily as a trail of corruption and degeneration. Perhaps the road back, to the past, won't miss the chance of turning into a trail of cleansing from the damages committed by futures, whenever they turned into a present?' (2017, Introduction).

We have seen how, historically, ruins have often functioned as a vector for the feeling of nostalgia, eliciting rumination on loss and a now unreachable past. Ruins have been a constant source of nostalgia for times that have passed, an almost 'too easy and perhaps even too "cheap"' conduit of reflection on the perishability of human things and on the past: 'ruins actually really do have all the formal and emotional features that make them ideal candidates of becoming par excellence stimulators of nostalgia' (Somhegy 2024, 427). More than this, however, ruins are associated with pre-modern times. Nostalgia, as Svetlana Boym reminds us, 'is coeval with the birth of mass culture' (2002, Chapter One), and the origins of ruin lust can be found in the Grand Tour, which is to say, during the early Industrial Revolution, with which they have to be understood to be in dialogue. The same economic expansion and growing industrialization that were transforming European cities and countrysides fuelled an interest in, almost a need for, images of peaceful remnants of a world that had not yet been accelerated, urbanized, and globalized. Ruins, as we have seen, were perceived as cultural artefacts outside of time, separate from the violence that had produced them (Somhegy 2024, 429–30). In the age of *Ruinenlust*, as Svetlana Boym argues, ruins became part of an institutionalization of nostalgia: they became sites of national heritage, monumentalized versions of the past (2002, Chapter One), and yet, at the same time, in being perceived as peaceful and removed from contemporary changes and struggles, they also became historical artefacts somehow deprived of history.

In contemporary ruins, the feeling of nostalgia is even more accentuated as contemporary ruins involve buildings and objects that are close to us, that do not speak of a distant past but rather of a nearer one, strongly reminding us that ruination can occur to any of our spaces and artefacts. At the same time, contemporary ruins remind us of different ideas of the future: they are filled with promises, possibilities, and hopes that did not manifest themselves (Somhegy 2024, 433–4). The ruins of Detroit are not nostalgic simply because they are images of destruction but also because this destruction involves an idea of a future that never came to be. Detroit has become an image of ruination and decay in which human life is reduced and non-human agencies have found a new space in which to act; it is also a visual reflection of the imperial status that once seemed to be embedded in the city's fabric and future but that disappeared, very much like the promises of prosperity, wealth, and security of the retail ruins.

Nostalgia has been extensively theorized in relation to cinema and television, visual arts and tourism, and cultural heritage and politics.[9] Yet, despite the many ways in which it has been used, nostalgia has seldom been discussed in relation to ecology. Contemporary environmental discourse, however, is often nostalgic in its undertones. Nostalgia, including ecological nostalgia, is at the core of many touristic experiences (Ceisel 2018; Berliner 2020): just as ruin tourism offers the possibility of witnessing destruction without actually having to experience it first-hand, many of today's touristic experiences are predicated on seeing pristine landscapes and experiencing pre-modern ways of life without having to renounce the comforts of modernity and the benefits of a globalized economy, or at least only having to renounce them temporarily.

This nostalgic image of a pre-modern world is common in popular ecological discourse. During the Covid-19 pandemic, for instance, a recurring kind of visual content started circulating. This involved images of various monuments and cities around the world that had been rendered less polluted or crowded by the forced seclusion imposed by the disease, accompanied by the sentence 'nature is healing' (which, of course, quickly turned into a meme, with all kinds of humorous reprises). In those images, the water in Venice's canals becoming clear again was a sign that, indeed, nature was 'healing', a sentence that implied, however, that the human species was a disease. Crucially, the 'nature is healing' meme manifested itself at a time when the planet was suffering one of the worst crises in recent times – a crisis of a kind that has been incessantly dramatized in post-apocalyptic fantasies – thereby immediately activating the imagery of ruins: nature can 'heal' only among the remnants of human civilization.

This is a common trope in current environmental populism, which, paired with the idea of a nostalgic 'return to nature', discerns an essential opposition between human culture and natural elements, and identifies a solution to current environmental problems in the return to a pre-modern way of life. While many ecosystems suffer under the pressure of human activity, such approaches identify humanity as something entirely external to the natural world, and not a part of it. Most importantly, it seems that only through the disappearance of the human species can 'nature' finally 'heal'. This kind of discourse, partly humorous and partly not, is indicative of a certain tendency in ecological thinking that goes hand in hand with other regressive tendencies like neo-ruralism or primitivism. Reflecting on ecology often means thinking about simpler times – not about a sustainable future, but about a romanticized past in which the human

---

[9] In addition to what is quoted directly here, on nostalgia in contemporary culture, see Dika 2003; Reynolds 2011; Cassin 2013; Cross 2015; Becker 2023.

species has not yet had such an impact on the planet's environments. Similarly, the 'memefication' of environmental terrorist Ted Kaczynski (also known as the Unabomber), whose mugshot is often humorously paired with news about automatization and pollution, is indicative of this tendency.

Thus, it is no coincidence that early discussions of ecocriticism focused on the pastoral genre, a literary and visual form (often connected to romanticized portraits of ruins) in which natural landscapes are idealized in opposition to modernity: the pastoral itself functioned as a genre in which environmental concerns and reflections on the relationship between nature and culture could be depicted. Lawrence Buell opened his pioneering *The Environmental Imagination* with the assertion: 'I start with the subject of pastoral, for "pastoral" has become almost synonymous with the idea of (re)turn to a less urbanized, more "natural" state of existence. Indeed, this entire book, in focusing on art's capacity to image and remythify the natural environment, is itself a kind of pastoral project' (1995, 31). Today, nostalgia is often part of a similar ecological stance. Primitivism and the idea of a 'return to nature' represent similar 'pastoral projects' in their attempt to imagine a world from which modernity has simply, almost magically, disappeared. However, compared to Buell's seminal study, more recent approaches to the pastoral have focused on its ambiguous dimension. According to Heather I. Sullivan, the pastoral is a mode that, on the one hand, was predicated on the opposition between the city and the countryside, tradition and modernity, and that, on the other hand, did not recognize the continuity between those spaces and the processes at play in them: 'the traditional forms of pastoral ... can attain their most poetic aspects precisely by overlooking, ignoring, and deceptively painting over human power struggles for land, control over species, economic practices, and exploitation of others' (Sullivan 2017, 29).

In an age of increasing environmental instability and violence, as well as alienation from the natural world, feelings of nostalgia in relation to a more sustainable lifestyle can only be expected to grow. Sullivan has talked about a 'dark pastoral' as an iteration of this mode that is specific to the Anthropocene and addresses 'the darkness of our rapidly growing knowledge about industrial cultures' tainted tactics when accessing and using "natural resources" and the standard obliviousness to the resultant waste' (2017, 26). In a dark pastoral mode, ruins are no longer the peaceful setting of gatherings of shepherds, as in traditional ruin painting, but something simultaneously more sinister and more active. In a similar way, Niklas Salmose and Anna Ishchenko have addressed the issue of an 'Anthropocene nostalgia' – an ecological vision associated with a sense of 'total loss' (2024, 237) that is intrinsically connected to imagery of collapse and ruination, as global anthropogenic climate change and environmental disasters have altered and are altering the planet to such an extent that many familiar sights have been rendered unrecognizable. Moreover, 'eco-nostalgias encompass significantly more traumatic experiences that do not necessarily imply embodied displacement' (Angé and Berliner 2021, 5); they not only comprise traditional ruins but also the condition of living with the perils of water contamination and radioactivity, as we have seen in relation to Fukushima and West Virginia.

That nostalgia is an ambiguous political tool is signalled by the fact that, unlike memory and history, it does not create a shared community, but rather links individuals on the basis of interests, thereby forming groups but not societies (Cross 2015, 14). It is, in other words, a self-referential feeling that manifests itself in consumption rather than action, and that ends up having an incapacitating effect. Ryan Lizardi underlines the intrinsic narcissism of contemporary culture, which is founded on a movement that is private and personal, as if the historical horizon were reduced to the much narrower horizon of personal experience (Lizardi 2015, 12). This ambiguity extends to Anthropocene nostalgia as well. On the one hand, responses to Anthropocenic violence can turn to denialism or facile, individualistic solutions. Climate denialism can be read, to a certain extent, as a nostalgic reaction, insofar as it refuses to acknowledge the changes occurring on the planet, and it imposes an outdated, idealized view of our relationship with the environment on the harsh reality of the Anthropocene (Salmose and Ishchenko 2024, 239). On the other hand, thinking about the past of the environment also means thinking about alternatives, about the idea that other relationships with it are possible, and contributes to creating a connection between individual and social practices (Salmose and Ishchenko 2024, 239). Ruins reflect this scenario in their ambiguity: they are simultaneously images of loss and symbols of alternative genealogies of our relationship with planetary environments.

4.2 'An architecture of broken dreams': Retail Ruins and Semiotic Ghosts

Among contemporary ruins, those that evoke more nostalgia are the ones Jacob C. Miller calls 'retail ruin[s]', meaning '"dead" or "zombie" shopping malls, sputtering high streets, vanishing department stores and other scenes of vacancy, abandonment, dereliction and disarray' (2023, 1). Retail ruins are a peculiar kind of contemporary ruin, one that does not belong to either the sphere of the familiar or the public sphere, but rather one in between that encompasses consumption and entertainment. Retail ruins are spaces that were simultaneously privately owned and crowded with the public dreams of consumerism; in them, it is possible to see both the uncanny memory of the entertainment of the past, and a reflection on the limits and perils of consumerism. Such ruins 'illuminate in a troubling way how *even that landscape, the landscape of spectacle, can fall into ruin*' (Miller 2023, 1).

We have already mentioned the idea that, in ruins, chronologies collapse and are confounded. In this sense, ruins have 'hauntological capacities', Miller argues, referring to Derrida's concept of hauntology, a playful yet revealing crasis of 'haunting' and 'ontology' that seeks to describe the spectral nature of contemporary culture (on ruins and haunting, see also Trigg 2009). Heavily reused by cultural critics like Mark Fisher (2014), hauntology refers to the superimposition of different chronological planes onto today's culture and our experience of it, and extensively deals with the concept of nostalgia permeating present-day cultural production. In the case of ruins, it refers to the ways in which they simultaneously address the past, the present, and the future, thereby eliciting a wide variety of responses from us: 'the retail ruin produces potentially complicated affective and emotional scenes for a populace that relies on the retail landscape for any number of purposes' (Miller 2023, 5). Such confusion is powerful.

In this sense, retail ruins are akin to the 'semiotic ghosts' at the centre of William Gibson's short story 'The Gernsback Continuum' (1981): they are filled with images and remnants of a future that could have been an economic model that promised wealth and endless wonder and that is now in decay (see Wood 2021, 3–6). The title refers to Hugo Gernsback, editor of seminal sci-fi magazines like *Amazing Stories*; it is simultaneously a tongue-in-cheek reference for the fandom and a commentary on the capability of science fiction to produce images of the future. As the summary accompanying the short story asked, 'how would you feel if those futurescapes of fifty years ago materialized today?' Indeed, how do we feel when those futurescapes materialize in the images of retail ruins? 'The Gernsback Continuum' follows the narrator and protagonist, a photographer working on a project about architecture in the 1930s and 1940s, as he starts having visions of the future as it was conceived in those decades, featuring flying cars, airships, and so on. Images of the past future, in other words, are superimposed onto those of the present and its promises. One of his employers describes this aesthetic as 'raygun Gothic', and envisions it as 'as a kind of alternate America: a 1980 that never happened. An architecture of broken dreams' (Gibson 2010). 'Architecture of broken dreams' is a definition that aptly summarizes the notion of retail ruins, spaces built to accommodate the needs of a rapidly growing and increasingly wealthy society that did not live up to the promises it was making. At the same time, the expression recalls Friedrich's dreamer, whose oneiric fantasies have now been shattered by the frenzy of modernity.

Semiotic ghosts, according to the protagonist's contact, are 'bits of deep cultural imagery that have split off and taken on a life of their own, like the Jules Verne airships that those old Kansas farmers were always seeing. But you saw a different kind of ghost, that's all'; these ghosts once belonged to the 'mass unconscious' and are now embedded in individual consciousness as well (Gibson 2010). The protagonist hallucinates and sees the 'secret ruins' of this future that never was:

> And that was my frame of mind as I made the stations of her convoluted socioarchitectural cross in my red Toyota – as I gradually tuned in to her image of a shadowy America-that-wasn't, of Coca-Cola plants like beached submarines, and fifth-run movie houses like the temples of some lost sect that had worshiped blue mirrors and geometry. And as I moved among these secret ruins, I found myself wondering what the inhabitants of that lost future would think of the world I lived in. The Thirties dreamed white marble and slipstream chrome, immortal crystal and burnished bronze, but the rockets on the covers of the Gernsback pulps had fallen on London in the dead of night, screaming. After the war, everyone had a car – no wings for it – and the promised superhighway to drive it down, so that the sky itself darkened, and the fumes ate the marble and pitted the miracle crystal. (Gibson 2010)

The promises of the future encapsulated by this vision are more fascinating, more inviting, than the present in which the protagonist lives, and he has to resort to numbing himself with violent news and sordid pornography to get rid of them. In their perfection and peacefulness, which contradict the reality of the world as it really developed, they elicit a sense of nostalgia, the idea that things were once, or at least could have been, different from the way they are now.

Something similar happens in retail ruins: from an environmental perspective, more than other human artefacts, retail ruins are a symbol of the unsustainability of contemporary culture and the promises of endless growth it makes. In everyday language, malls are usually referred to as 'temples of consumerism'; in a certain way, they are a continuation of the ruins of actual temples and churches that were immortalized in Romantic and Gothic art (Somhegyi 2020, 114). Like temples and churches, retail ruins are not just symbols of consumerism but also symbols of a specific urbanistic model. Built from the 1950s onwards outside city centres in order to be easily accessible by car and to create shopping opportunities for the inhabitants of the suburbs (Somhegyi 2020, 113–4), malls are one of the epitomes of a culture based on automobile transport. The growing number of mall ruins (especially after the 2008 economic crisis, the Covid-19 pandemic, and the competition of e-commerce sites), scattered across residential areas, reflects not only the downfall of an economic model predicated on consumption and the endless acquisition of superfluous and replaceable goods but also the ways in which our societies are increasingly deterritorialized. Malls are one of the most distinct examples of what Marc Augé has described as 'non-places' (1992), meaning the non-descriptive, anonymous spaces of contemporary capitalism, spaces with which no deep emotional relationship, no sense of historical depth, is possible. As in the case of Detroit, it is not the engine of progress that jammed, but the economy, forcing commercial spaces to close and move elsewhere, aggravating the isolation of individuals and their dependency on commercial oligopolies. Yet, precisely for this reason, the ruins of malls also have the power to unsettle us, to remind us that, while they originally appeared to be outside of space and time, paradoxically frozen in the continuous and overwhelming circulation of goods, malls are subject to decay as well: 'the derelict shopping malls ... are disquieting not only because they mark the end of a dream or are still too close to our time to attain the classical noble patina ..., but also because we feel a bit impotent, powerless, and even helpless when observing these sites' (Somhegyi 2020, 120). It is the same feeling of impotence that the protagonists of *It Follows* experience: the feeling of fighting against something that, like the ghostly economy generating and then dismantling the mall phenomenon, is everywhere, and answers to a logic of its own.

Unsurprisingly, considering the extent to which the series is devoted to the representation of decay, retail ruins can be found in *The Last of Us*. Episode 7 ('Left Behind', a title that shares the semantics of ruins) is almost entirely set in an abandoned mall, in a long flashback in which the female protagonist, the teenager Ellie, visits an abandoned mall with her friend and love interest, another young woman named Riley. After a night spent wandering among the remnants of the shops and entertainment sites of the mall, the two are attacked by an infected, and are both bitten – and while Ellie turns out to be immune to the contagion, her friend succumbs. In this episode (which, in a further nostalgic twist, recalls familiar mall-based zombie movies like Romero's *Dawn of the Dead*, 1978), viewers are offered the estranging perspective of seeing parts of their everyday lives (escalators, franchises like Footlocker or Victoria's Secret, arcade video games) turned into precious remnants of a lost past.

The ruins of consumerism depicted here are meant to convey a sense of impermanence, while simultaneously complicating the status of what our culture produces. Ellie's friend refers to the highlights of the mall as 'wonders', and takes her there with the intent of showing her five of them: a clear reference to the classical tradition of the 'seven wonders' of the world, also reprised by Weisman in his book (chapter 12 is titled 'The Fate of the Ancient and Modern Wonders of the World'). The classical tradition, however, is centred on vast monuments, while in the episode the 'wonders' are banal objects and spaces, such as the arcade and the carousel. The choice of setting of the episode in the mall highlights a contradictory feature of retail ruins: they are not the eternal remnants of something built to last, but rather the discarded remains of a commodity-fuelled economy and landscape. Yet, in becoming ruins, these spaces also acquire a sense of historical depth that, as non-places, they did not possess when they were active. Retail ruins function therefore as both a symbol of the caducity of capitalist culture, and a re-semantization of the non-places of capitalism into spaces that are inherently imbued with history.

At the same time, ruins are a spectral manifestation of a past that does not exist anymore, but remains to haunt the present. Crucial to this conceptualization of ruins is the fact that, in the episode, the mall serves as a space of exploration of queer sexualities, as it allows the development of the relationship between Ellie and her friend, which would be impossible in the authoritarian governmental regime that rules the community of survivors. In this sense, the mall functions as an example of 'queer nostalgia' (Padva) – a repurposing of a past that consistently excluded queer voices as a space where they can manifest themselves and be heard. If nostalgia, as Gilad Padva writes in relation to queerness, 'creates an emotional landscape, a sentimental environment that cherishes past experiences, whether these are personal or communal occurrences' (2014, 3), then 'reinventing or retelling the past is a major part of the creation of a gay, lesbian, bisexual, and transgender heritage with its own role models, icons, symbols, emblems, and glorified imageries' (2014, 6). Through nostalgia, the past is rendered queer by means of the creation of a non-linear and multipolar genealogy (2014, 7) that, lacking direct models, recovers those of a shared past and re-semantizes them in a queer fashion. This is precisely what happens in *The Last of Us*, in which the mall and the elements of pop culture within it create a space where the queerness of the protagonists can manifest. This manifestation is only possible thanks to the transformation of the mall into the empty, blank space of a ruin, but this transformation is also what signals its dangerousness: the infected hidden in the abandoned mall serves as a warning against the comfort of nostalgia. The association of nostalgia with ruins is meant as a comment on the incapacitating nature of nostalgia in contemporary culture: the mall represents a moment of escapism, but also tragedy.

This individual dimension is not disconnected from an environmental perspective. Retails ruins and semiotic ghosts do not simply comment on our fascination with the past and a nostalgia for a time when the future appeared to be brighter, but also reflect the uneasiness and difficulty of living on an increasingly dangerous planet. Ellie's retreat into the uncomplicated, yet treacherous, past of the mall, with its oneiric fantasies of overabundance, is not dissimilar to the retreat into primitivist fantasies. They are a manifestation, in other words, of what we called Anthropocene nostalgia – a nostalgia that differs to that of the pastoral mode, but is still relevant to current environmental discourse. Ellie's incursion into the ruined mall is an escape from an overwhelming post-apocalyptic present just as fantasies of a 'return to nature' are an escape from our overly polluted and exploited present. Furthermore, like the ruins of Detroit, retail ruins force us to confront the volatility of our economic system, including its globalized and yet delocalized dimension.

4.3 'Look on my works, ye Mighty, and despair!'

The ambiguous status of ruins in contemporary science fiction, as seen in *The Last of Us*, reflects the ambiguity with which our culture receives them today: as spaces of openness and encounter with other agencies that can, however, take on a nightmarish dimension; as spaces in which different paths to the future can be considered; and as the remnants of an incapacitating past from which no life can come. From an environmental perspective, this ambiguity reflects that of the apocalyptic mode as a tool of ecological discussion. The anthropomorphism of ruins, which we have already mentioned in relation to the Statue of Liberty, can be found in *Blade Runner 2049* (2017) as well. Compared to *Blade Runner* (1982), the sequel recovers the more explicitly post-apocalyptic dimension of Philip K. Dick's novella. In *Do Androids Dream of Electric Sheep?*, Earth is described as a post-apocalyptic planet from which, following a 'World War Terminus' fought with atomic weapons, most people have escaped, leaving behind the physically and mentally disabled or those with a specific (economic) interest in staying on the dying planet. In Scott's adaptation, the apocalyptic element is transformed into a dystopian setting, which is reprised in turn in *Blade Runner 2049*. This movie, however, also incorporates a more explicitly post-apocalyptic sequence set in Las Vegas, rendered uninhabitable following a nuclear fallout. The sequence follows the protagonist, the android K, as he searches for Deckard, the protagonist of the previous movie, played once again by an aged Harrison Ford.

While travelling to the abandoned hotel where Deckard lives, K ventures into a ruined landscape, in which everything is engulfed in a cloud of orange dust – suggesting the persistent effects of radiation on the area, thereby making the invisible visible, as we have seen in Vollmann. The first human artefacts we see are huge statues that used to welcome the tourists and are now deformed and scarred, reduced to silhouettes – an almost literal rendition of Percy Shelley's famous lines 'on the sand, / half sunk a shattered visage lies' (vv. 3–4; see Figure 8). Contrary to other depictions of ruins, and in keeping with the desert setting of the city, the ruined buildings are not represented as devoured by

Figure 8 Frame from *Blade Runner 2049* (2017), dir. Denis Villeneuve.

Figure 9 Frame from *Blade Runner 2049* (2017), dir. Denis Villeneuve.

vegetation, but rather isolated in a sort of perpetual stillness that contrasts with their decayed status. When K enters the hotel, the scenery is that of an abandoned place, in which the objects of everyday life (tables and chairs, a piano, the bottles at a bar) are left untouched, but whose disarray signals their new status as ruins.

The desertic climate of Las Vegas prevents the hotel's ruins from becoming engulfed in vegetation; yet the topos of ruins as a space of meeting with non-human agencies is still present in K's encounter with bees, a surprisingly pastoral moment in what is otherwise an exceptionally pessimistic film. Among the statues, K notices a beehive, likely planted there by Deckard (see Figure 9). The empty space of Las Vegas stands in contrast to the crowded cities in which most of the rest of the movie is set, and the presence of insects refers to one of the crucial themes of both the movies and, even more so, Dick's novella, which pivots on the notion of mass extinction and questioning the human–animal divide (Vint 2010, 30–32; Jørgensen 2022). By representing animal farming in a ruined landscape, Villeneuve is hinting not only at the centuries-long tradition of representations of shepherds among classical ruins (a pastoral trope) but also at the positive value of such scenery. Although the whole movie lacks actual animals, and it has been pointed out that 'the buzzing of the colonies is perhaps the first animal sound in the entire film' (Sarvis-Wilburn 2018), the portrayal of animal farming (and especially animals like bees, whose disappearance is usually considered an alarming sign of environmental collapse) is a reference to a regenerating function of ruins, which counters the frenzy of modernity. It is, in other words, a nostalgic scene in which a more balanced relationship with the environment is possible only because of the retreat of humankind. At the same time, the viewer is left to wonder what kind of life is possible among ruins – and what kind of life can bees lead in a desert, where there is no sign of vegetal life (it might even be the case that the bees, like most of the animals in Dick's novella, are artificial). If ruins here appear as a space of openness and calm, and even the possible re-establishment of an equilibrium between human and non-human life, it is a life that is inherently diminished.

The second function of ruins in the movie is to reinforce one of its central issues, that of paternity. K is seeking Deckard because he believes he is his father: a miraculous birth among replicants that might signal the beginning of a new species. Later, in his search for the truth, K finds out that it was not Deckard who fathered him, but another person. Crucially, their confrontation (a fistfight) takes place in the ruined hotel, in which holograms of past celebrities are constantly playing their songs (see Figure 10) – veritable 'semiotic ghosts' superimposed on the protagonists of the movie, very much like the spectre of the original film is superimposed on *Blade Runner 2024*. Here ruins serve as a critical commentary on the nostalgic function that is traditionally associated with them. In this sense, the ruins of Las Vegas perfectly encapsulate retail

Figure 10 Frame from *Blade Runner 2049* (2017), dir. Denis Villeneuve.

ruins' hauntological capacities: the holograms inhabiting the abandoned casino like spectres evoke the incapacitating persistence of the past in the present, and the inability of the present to produce something new – a reflection that is enhanced by the meta-commentary of the film, which is a sequel to a movie from the 1980s and has some of the same actors. While viewers ultimately find out that replicants did indeed produce offspring, K's dream of having a father is frustrated; similarly, ruins appear to have lost their productive, generative power for the human race; they can only serve as a shelter for sparse animal life that cannot find space elsewhere.

The Las Vegas segment of *Blade Runner 2049* encapsulates the sublime dimension of Anthropocene violence as a reflection of the perils of human activities – in this case, nuclear energy. Like Vollmann in Fukushima, K moves across a landscape that has been devastated by a disaster caused by human activity, while simultaneously confronting the unlikely survival of non-human agencies and the residual agency of the disaster itself in the form of radiation. Despite suggesting peace, then, ruins appear once again as anything but peaceful: they are much more complicated and active artefacts than traditional depictions of them might lead us to believe. At the same time, the casino into which K ventures is a properly hauntological space, intertwined with alternative chronologies and promises of a different future that are closely tied to the character's failed dreams of paternity. This crucial ambivalence in relation to ruins, as we have seen, characterizes their representation in contemporary culture at large.

Conclusion: The State of Things to Come

Throughout this Element, I have argued that ruins reflect a sense of precariousness: they function as material proof of the fact that nothing lasts forever and that all things perish and, most importantly, transform. It is in this sense that, in the Introduction to this work, we defined ruins, quoting Andrew F. Wood, as 'a rhetoric of things to come' (2021, xii); or, to reprise the quote by the Italian band Shores of Null that opens this Element, ruins are 'the state of things to come'. This is the key, elementary truth about ruins, the memento mori they represent in our eyes: when we see a ruin, we are viewing what the spaces and places we inhabit and love will become. Yet, this does not explain or exhaust the power ruins have in contemporary culture. We have seen how ruins are one of the manifestations of the Anthropocene sublime, that is, a symbol of the effects of vast, non-human agencies and chronologies whose danger is, however, caused by human activity. We have seen, too, how ruins contradictorily fuel a sense of nostalgia for simpler, non-Anthropocenic times, or the possibilities these times promised. Ruins are also, however, (eco)Gothic artefacts, spaces open to the return of the environmentally removed and repressed and the manifestation of the agencies of the non-human world – a return that can take reassuring or nightmarish forms, depending on who is dreaming of it. It is in this sense that we have discussed ruins in light of a negative ecology, a kind of ecological thought that values the discarded and the marginal, the uncanny and the spectral, the disturbing and the terrifying. Thinking with ruins implies paying attention to things that are overlooked in our environments, recognizing their potential, and noticing the innumerable agencies at play around us: it implies favouring alternative visions and genealogies, addressing our own past and the weight it still has in our societies and industrial systems, and changing the ways in which we act and move in the world.

As its subtitle suggests, this Element has been a long exercise in environmental imagination – that is, an attempt to interact with one key constituent of our environmentally oriented cultural imagery, and to contribute to complicating it. Analysing cultural artefacts is important not only because it is through culture (and especially popular culture) that we can truly understand how things are perceived but also because they influence our perception and understanding of phenomena. Exercises in environmental imagination are thus necessary not simply to gather knowledge about reality in increasingly worrysome times but also, more importantly, to create the conceptual tools to address the countless issues we are currently facing. The humanities are often seen as impractical or even useless in the face of the enormous environmental crises of the present, but I argue that the opposite is the case: if it is true that, as William Cronon says, nature is a cultural concept (1996), then it is only through a discussion of culture and its material and immaterial manifestations that we can change our relationship with the environment. At its core, this Element attempts to do that, and to embrace the change in values and perceptions that comes with adopting a negative ecology. Ruins are the shape of things to come, but we are not powerless in creating this shape.

References

Alaimo, S. (2016). *Exposed. Environmental Politics and Pleasures in Posthuman Times*. Minneapolis: University of Minnesota Press.

Angé, O., and Berliner, D. (2021). Introduction. In O. Angé and D. Berliner, eds., *Ecological Nostalgias Memory, Affect and Creativity in Times of Ecological Upheavals*. New York: Berghahn Books, pp. 1–16.

Apel, D. (2015). *Beautiful Terrible Ruins: Detroit and the Anxiety of Decline*. New Brunswick, NJ: Rutgers University Press.

Armiero, M. (2021). *Wasteocene: Stories from the Global Dump*. Cambridge: Cambridge University Press.

Augé, M. (1992). *Non-Lieux. Introduction à une anthropologie de la surmodernité*. Paris: Éditions du Seuil.

Augé, M. (2003). *Le temps en ruines*. Paris: Éditions Galilée.

Austin, D. and Doerr, S. (2010). *Lost Detroit: Stories Behind the Motor City's Majestic Ruins*. Cheltenham: The History Press.

Bauman, Z. (2017). *Retrotopia*. Cambridge: Polity. Epub.

Becker, T. (2023). *Yesterday: A New History of Nostalgia*. Cambridge, MA: Harvard University Press.

Benjamin, W. (2019). *Origin of the German Trauerspiel*. Translated by Howard Eiland. Cambridge, MA: Harvard University Press.

Berliner, D. (2020). *Losing Culture: Nostalgia, Heritage, and Our Accelerated Times*. Translated by D. Horsfall. New Brunswick, NJ: Rutgers University Press.

Binelli, M. (2012). *Detroit City Is the Place to Be: The Afterlife of an American Metropolis*. New York: Metropolitan Books.

Bingham, K. P. (2020). *An Ethnography of Urban Exploration: Unpacking Heterotopic Social Space*. London: Palgrave.

Borsari, A. (2022). On the Aesthetics of the Anthropocene: The Sublime and Beyond – Other Concepts and Forms of Visualizations. *European Journal of Creative Practices in Cities and Landscapes*, 5(2), 242–58.

Boym, S. (2002). *The Future of Nostalgia*. New York: Basic Books. Epub.

Brady, E. (2012). The Environmental Sublime. In T. M. Costelloe, ed., *The Sublime: From Antiquity to the Present*. Cambridge: Cambridge University Press, pp. 171–182.

Buell, L. (1995). *The Environmental Imagination: Thoreau, Nature Writing, and the Formation of American Culture*. Cambridge, MA: Harvard University Press.

Burke, E. (1998). *A Philosophical Enquiry*. Edited by Adam Phillips. Oxford: Oxford University Press.

Byron, G. G. (1819). 'Ode on Venice'. https://en.wikisource.org/wiki/Mazeppa,_a_Poem/Ode.

Camara, A. (2014). Abominable Transformations: Becoming-Fungus in Arthur Machen's *The Hill of Dreams*. *Gothic Studies*, 16(1), 9–23.

Caracciolo, M. (2021). Being Moved by Nature in the Anthropocene: On the Limits of the Ecological Sublime. *Emotion Review*, 13(4), 299–305.

Cassin, B. (2013). *La nostalgie: Quand donc est-on chez soi? Ulysse, Énée, Arendt*. Paris: Éditions Autrement.

Ceisel, C. M. (2018). *Globalized Nostalgia: Tourism, Heritage, and the Politics of Place*. New York: Routledge.

Chakrabarty, D. (2009). The Climate of History: Four Theses. *Critical Inquiry*, 35, 197–222.

Church, D. (2021). *Post-Horror: Art, Genre, and Cultural Elevation*. Edinburgh: Edinburgh University Press.

Cohen, J. J. (2015). *Stone: An Ecology of the Inhuman*. Minneapolis: University of Minnesota Press.

Cronon, W. (1996). The Trouble with Wilderness: Or, Getting Back to the Wrong Nature. *Environmental History*, 1(1), 7–28.

Cross, G. (2015). *Consumed Nostalgia: Memory in the Age of Fast Capitalism*. New York: Columbia University Press.

Derrida, J. (1993). *Spectres de Marx: l'état de la dette, le travail du deuil et la nouvelle Internationale*. Paris: Éditions Galilée.

Dika, V. (2003). *Recycled Culture in Contemporary Art and Film: The Uses of Nostalgia*. Cambridge: Cambridge University Press.

Dillon, B. (2011). *Ruins*. Cambridge, MA: The MIT Press.

Dobraszczyk, P. (2015). *The Dead City: Urban Ruins and the Spectacle of Decay*. London: I.B. Tauris.

Doran, R. (2015). *The Theory of the Sublime from Longinus to Kant*. Cambridge: Cambridge University Press.

Douglas, M. (2001). *Purity and Danger: An Analysis of Concepts of Pollution and Taboo*. New York: Routledge.

Edensor, T. (2005). *Industrial Ruins: Spaces, Aesthetics and Materiality*. London: Bloomsbury.

Edwards, J. D., Graulund, R., and Höglund, J. (2022). Introduction: Gothic in the Anthropocene. In J. D. Edwards, R. Graulund, and J. Höglund, eds., *Dark Scenes from Damaged Earth: The Gothic Anthropocene*. Minneapolis: University of Minnesota Press, pp. ix–xxvi.

Eliot, G. (2000). *Middlemarch*. Edited by Bert G. Hornback. New York: Norton.

Estok, S. C. (2020). *The Ecophobia Hypothesis*. New York: Routledge.

Estok, S. C. (2025). *Slime: An Elemental Imagery*. Cambridge: Cambridge University Press.

Ferguson, F. (1984). The Nuclear Sublime. *Diacritics*, 14(2), 4–10.

Ferrante, A. A. (2022). *Cosa può un compost: Fare con le ecologie femministe e queer*. Roma: Luca Sossella Editore.

Fisher, M. (2014). *Ghosts of My Life: Writings on Depression, Hauntology and Lost Futures*. Winchester, KY: Zero Books.

Foley, M., and Lennon, J. J. (1996). JFK and Dark Tourism: A Fascination with Assassination. *International Journal of Heritage Studies*, 2(4), 198–211.

Gibson, W. (2010). *Burning Chrome*. New York: Voyager Books. Epub.

Glotfelty, C. (2014). Corporeal Fieldwork and Risky Art: Peter Goin and the Making of *Nuclear Landscapes*. In S. Iovino and S. Oppermann, eds., *Material Ecocriticism*. Bloomington: Indiana University Press, pp. 221–238.

Goatcher, J., and Brunsden, V. (2011). Chernobyl and the Sublime Tourist. *Tourist Studies*, 11(2), 115–37.

Hamilton, J. M., and Neimanis, A. (2018). Composting Feminism and Environmental Humanities. *Environmental Humanities*, 10/2, 502–27.

Haraway, D. (2016). *Staying with the Trouble: Making Kin in the Chthulucene*. Durham, NC: Duke University Press.

Harbison, R. (2015). *Ruins and Fragments: Tales of Loss and Rediscovery*. London: Reaktion Books.

Hatherley, O. (2010). *A Guide to the New Ruins of Great Britain*. London: Verso.

Hell, J. (2010). Imperial Ruin Gazers, or Why Did Scipio Weep? In J. Hell and A. Schönle, eds., *Ruins of Modernity*. Durham, NC: Duke University Press, pp. 169–192.

Hell, J., and Schönle, A. (2010). Introduction. In J. Hell and A. Schönle, eds., *Ruins of Modernity*. Durham, NC: Duke University Press, pp. 1–14.

Hitt, C. (1999). Toward an Ecological Sublime. *New Literary History*, 30(3), 603–23.

Hurley, J. (2020). *Infrastructures of Apocalypse: American Literature and the Nuclear Complex*. Minneapolis: University of Minnesota Press.

Huyssen, A. (2010). Authentic Ruins: Products of Modernity. In J. Hell and A. Schönle, eds., *Ruins of Modernity*. Durham, NC: Duke University Press, pp. 17–28.

Ibata, H. (2018). *The Challenge of the Sublime from Burke's Philosophical Enquiry to British Romantic Art*. Manchester: Manchester University Press.

Iovino, S., and Oppermann, S. (2014). Introduction: Stories Come to Matter. In S. Iovino and S. Oppermann, eds., *Material Ecocriticism*. Bloomington: Indiana University Press, pp. 1–17.

Jackson, J. B. (1980). *The Necessity for Ruins and Other Topics*. Amherst: University of Massachusetts Press.

Jørgensen, D. (2022). Resurrecting Species through Robotics: Animal Extinction and Deextinction in Do Androids Dream of Electric Sheep? In S. Borkfelt and M. Stephan, eds., *Literary Animal Studies and the Climate Crisis*. London: Palgrave, pp. 229–243.

Kant, I. (2011). *Observations on the Feeling of the Beautiful and Sublime and Other Writings*. Edited by P. Frierson and P. Guyer. Cambridge: Cambridge University Press.

Keetley, D. (2016). Introduction: Six Theses on Plant Horror; or, Why Are Plants Horrifying? In D. Keetley and A. Tenga, eds., *Plant Horror: Approaches to the Monstrous Vegetal in Fiction and Film*. London: Palgrave Macmillan, pp. 1–30.

Keetley, D., and Sivils, M. W. (2017). Introduction: Approaches to the Ecogothic. In D. Keetley and M. W. Sivils, eds., *Ecogothic in Nineteenth-Century American Literature*. New York: Routledge, pp. 1–20.

Kelly, C. R. (2017). *It Follows*: Precarity, Thanatopolitics, and the Ambient Horror Film. *Critical Studies in Media Communication*, 34(3), 234–49.

Kinney, R. J. (2016). *Beautiful Wasteland. The Rise of Detroit as America's Postindustrial Frontier*. Minneapolis: University of Minnesota Press.

Latour, B. (2011). Waiting for Gaia: Composing the Common World through Arts and Politics. www.bruno-latour.fr/sites/default/files/124-GAIA-LONDON-SPEAP_0.pdf.

Light, D. (2017). Progress in Dark Tourism and Thanatourism Research: An Uneasy Relationship with Heritage Tourism. *Tourism Management*, 61, 275–301.

Lizardi, R. (2015). *Mediated Nostalgia: Individual Memory and Contemporary Mass Media*. Lanham, MD: Lexington Books.

Luisetti, F. (2023). *Nonhuman Subjects: An Ecology of Earth-Beings*. Cambridge: Cambridge University Press.

Lyons, S., ed. (2018). *Ruin Porn and the Obsession with Decay*. London: Palgrave.

Macaulay, R. (1953). *Pleasure of Ruins*. London: Thames & Hudson.

Marchand, Y., and Meffre, R. (2010). *The Ruins of Detroit*. Göttingen: Steidl.

Mariani, M. A. (2022). *Italian Literature in the Nuclear Age: A Poetics of the Bystander*. Oxford: Oxford University Press.

Marshall, B. M. (2021). *Industrial Gothic: Workers, Exploitation and Urbanization in Transatlantic Nineteenth-Century Literature*. Chicago: The University of Chicago Press.

Martini, A., and Sharma, N. (2022). Framing the Sublime as Affect in Post-Disaster Tourism. *Annals of Tourism Research*, 97.

Masco, J. (2021). *The Future of Fallout, and Other Episodes in Radioactive World-Making*. Durham, NC: Duke University Press.

McGrath, S. J. (2019). *Thinking Nature: An Essay in Negative Ecology*. Edinburgh: Edinburgh University Press.

Miller, J. C. (2023). *Retail Ruins: The Ghosts of Post-Industrial Spectacle*. Bristol: Bristol University Press.

Moore, A. (2010). The Phoenix and the Pheasants. In A. Moore, ed., *Detroit Disassembled*. Bologna: Damiani Editore, pp. 118–119.

Morton, T. (2013). *Hyperobjects. Philosophy and Ecology after the End of the World*. Minneapolis: University of Minnesota Press.

Morton, T. (2018). *Dark Ecology: For a Logic of Future Coexistence*. New York: Columbia University Press.

Nixon, R. (2011). *Slow Violence and the Environmentalism of the Poor*. Cambridge, MA: Harvard University Press.

Orlando, F. (2006). *Obsolete Objects in the Literary Imagination: Ruins, Relies, Rarities, Rubbish, Uninhabited Places, and Hidden Treasures*. Translated from the Italian by Gabriel Pihas and Daniel Seidel, with the collaboration of Alessandra Grego. New Haven, CT: Yale University Press.

Orvell, M. (2013). Photographing Disaster: Urban Ruins and the Destructive Sublime. *Amerikastudien / American Studies*, 58(4), 647–71.

Orvell, M. (2021). *Empire of Ruins: American Culture, Photography, and the Spectacle of Destruction*. Oxford: Oxford University Press.

Padva, G. (2014). *Queer Nostalgia in Cinema and Pop Culture*. London: Palgrave.

Pétursdóttir, Þ., and Olsen, B. (2014a). Imaging Modern Decay: The Aesthetics of Ruin Photography. *Journal of Contemporary Archaeology*, 1(1), 7–23.

Pétursdóttir, Þ., and Olsen, B., eds. (2014b). *Ruin Memories: Materialities, Aesthetics and the Archaeology of the Recent Past*. New York: Routledge.

Piccini, A. (2014). Profane Archaeologies: Erotic Ruins and a Case for Pornography. *Journal of Contemporary Archaeology*, 1(1), 29–33.

Porter, J. I. (2011). Sublime Monuments and Sublime Ruins in Ancient Aesthetics. *European Review of History: Revue europeenne d'histoire*, 18 (5–6), 685–96.

Prica, A. (2022). *Decay and Afterlife: Form, Time, and the Textuality of Ruins, 1100 to 1900*. Chicago: The University of Chicago Press.

Punter, D. (1980). *The Literature of Terror*. London: Longman.

Ray, G. (2020). Terror and the Sublime in the So-Called Anthropocene. *Liminalities: A Journal of Performance Studies*, 16(2).

Regier, A. (2010). Foundational Ruins: The Lisbon Earthquake and the Sublime. In J. Hell and A. Schönle, eds., *Ruins of Modernity*. Durham, NC: Duke University Press, pp. 1–20.

Reynolds, S. (2011). *Retromania: Pop Culture's Addiction to Its Own Past.* London: Faber & Faber.

Rolfe, R. T., and Rolfe, F. W. (1974). *The Romance of the Fungus World.* Mineola, NY: Dover.

Salmose, N., and Ishchenko, A. (2024). Anthropocene Nostalgia. In T. Becker and D. Trigg, eds., *The Routledge Handbook of Nostalgia.* New York: Routledge, pp. 237–252.

Sarvis-Wilburn, M. (2018). The Dystopian Bees of *Blade Runner 2049. Bee Culture*, 23 March, www.beeculture.com/the-dystopian-bees-of-blade-runner-2049/.

Scanlan, J. (2005). *On Garbage.* London: Reaktion Books.

Shaw, P. (2006). *The Sublime.* New York: Routledge.

Shelley, P. B. (1819). Ozymandias. https://en.wikisource.org/wiki/Rosalind_and_Helen,_A_Modern_Eclogue_(1819)/Sonnet.

Simmel, G. (1958). Two Essays. *The Hudson Review*, 11(3), 371–85.

Skinner, J. (2018). 'The Smoke of an Eruption and the Dust of an Earthquake': Dark Tourism, the Sublime, and the Re-animation of the Disaster Location. In P. R. Stone, R. Hartmann, T. Seaton, R. Sharpley, and L. White, eds., *The Palgrave Handbook of Dark Tourism Studies.* London: Palgrave, pp. 125–150.

Somhegyi, Z. (2020). *Reviewing the Past: The Presence of Ruins.* Lanham, MD: Rowman and Littlefield.

Somhegyi, Z. (2024). Nostalgia and Ruins. In T. Becker and D. Trigg, eds., *The Routledge Handbook of Nostalgia.* New York: Routledge, pp. 427–439.

Stewart, S. (2020). *The Ruins Lessons: Meaning and Material in Western Culture.* Chicago: The University of Chicago Press.

Stoler, A. L. (2013). Introduction. 'The Rot Remains': From Ruins to Ruination. In A. L. Stoler, ed., *Imperial Debris: On Ruins and Ruination.* Durham, NC: Duke University Press, pp. 1–35.

Sullivan, H. I. (2017). The Dark Pastoral: A Trope for the Anthropocene. In C. Schaumann and H. I. Sullivan, eds., *German Ecocriticism in the Anthropocene.* London: Palgrave Macmillan, pp. 25–44.

Taylor, L. (2020). Rust Belt Ruins: The Gothic Genius Loci of Detroit. In H.-G. Millette and R. Heholt, eds., *The New Urban Gothic: Global Gothic in the Age of the Anthropocene.* London: Palgrave, pp. 149–163.

Trigg, D. (2009). The Place of Trauma: Memory, Hauntings, and the Temporality of Ruins. *Memory Studies*, 2(1), 87–101.

Trump, D. (transcribed by Politico Staff). (2017). Full Text: 2017 Donald Trump Inauguration Speech Transcript. *Politico*, 20 January, www.politico.com/story/2017/01/full-text-donald-trump-inauguration-speech-transcript-233907.

Tsing, A. L. (2015). *The Mushroom at the End of the World: On the Possibility of Life in Capitalist Ruins*. Princeton, NJ: Princeton University Press.

Tsing, A., Swanson, H., Gan, E., and Bubandt, N. (2017). Introduction: Haunted Landscapes of the Anthropocene. In A. Tsing, H. Swanson, E. Gan, and N. Bubandt, eds., *Arts of Living on a Damaged Planet*. Minneapolis: University of Minnesota Press, pp. 1–14.

Vint, S. (2010). *Animal Alterity: Science Fiction and the Question of the Animal*. Liverpool: Liverpool University Press.

Vollmann, W. T. (2018a). *Carbon Ideologies. Volume One: No Immediate Danger*. New York: Penguin Random House.

Vollmann, W. T. (2018b). *Carbon Ideologies. Volume Two: No Good Alternative*. New York: Penguin Random House.

Wagner, C. (2020). Risk, Invisibility, and Gothic Ruins in 2020: A Photo Essay. *Critical Quarterly*, 62(4), 63–73.

Weisman, A. (2007). *The World Without Us*. New York: Thomas Dunne Books.

Westling, L. (2022). *Deep History, Climate Change, and the Evolution of Human Culture*. Cambridge: Cambridge University Press.

Whitehouse, T. (2018). *How Ruins Acquire Aesthetic Value: Modern Ruins, Ruin Porn, and the Ruin Tradition*. London: Palgrave.

Wood, A. F. (2021). *A Rhetoric of Ruins: Exploring Landscapes of Abandoned Modernity*. Lanham: Lexington Books.

Zalasiewicz, J., Smith, A., Barry, T., and Coe, A.L. (2008). Are We Now Living in the Anthropocene? *GSA Today*, 18, 4–8.

Zucker, P. (1968). *Fascination of Decay: Ruins: Relic, Symbol, Ornament*. Ridgewood, NJ: Gregg Press.

Acknowledgements

I am grateful to the colleagues and friends who took the time to discuss this manuscript before it was submitted: Arianna Brunori, Anna Chiara Corradino, Costanza Geppert, Francesca Mavaracchio, and Stefano Serafini. The idea for this Element originated as an abstract for the special issue of *Ecozon@* edited by David Lombard, Alison Sperling, and Pieter Vermeulen: while I did not end up submitting an article, I wish to thank the editors for accepting the abstract and most importantly for prompting me to think about ruins in the first place. Finally, I am grateful to Michael Garvey for providing me with his proofreading services one last time: best of luck with your new career.

Cambridge Elements =

Environmental Humanities

Louise Westling
University of Oregon

Louise Westling is an American scholar of literature and environmental humanities who was a founding member of the Association for the Study of Literature and Environment and its President in 1998. She has been active in the international movement for environmental cultural studies, teaching and writing on landscape imagery in literature, critical animal studies, biosemiotics, phenomenology, and deep history.

Serenella Iovino
University of North Carolina at Chapel Hill

Serenella Iovino is Professor of Italian Studies and Environmental Humanities at the University of North Carolina at Chapel Hill. She has written on a wide range of topics, including environmental ethics and ecocritical theory, bioregionalism and landscape studies, ecofeminism and posthumanism, comparative literature, eco-art, and the Anthropocene.

Timo Maran
University of Tartu

Timo Maran is an Estonian semiotician and poet. Maran is Professor of Ecosemiotics and Environmental Humanities and Head of the Department of Semiotics at the University of Tartu. His research interests are semiotic relations of nature and culture, Estonian nature writing, zoosemiotics and species conservation, and semiotics of biological mimicry.

About the Series

The environmental humanities is a new transdisciplinary complex of approaches to the embeddedness of human life and culture in all the dynamics that characterize the life of the planet. These approaches reexamine our species' history in light of the intensifying awareness of drastic climate change and ongoing mass extinction. To engage this reality, Cambridge Elements in Environmental Humanities builds on the idea of a more hybrid and participatory mode of research and debate, connecting critical and creative fields.

Cambridge Elements

Environmental Humanities

Elements in the Series

Anthroposcreens: Mediating the Climate Unconscious
Julia Leyda

Aging Earth: Senescent Environmentalism for Dystopian Futures
Jacob Jewusiak

Blue Humanities: Storied Waterscapes in the Anthropocene
Serpil Oppermann

Nonhuman Subjects: An Ecology of Earth-Beings
Federico Luisetti

Indigenous Knowledge and Material Histories: The Example of Rubber
Jens Soentgen

The Open Veins of Modernity: Ecological Crisis and the Legacy of Byzantium and Pre-Columbian America
Eleni Kefala

Slime: An Elemental Imaginary
Simon C. Estok

Growing Hope: Narratives of Food Justice
Alexa Weik von Mossner

Descartes and the Non-human
Emma Gilby

Automobility and the Anthropocene: The Car as Post-Human
Gordon M. Sayre

The Earth Intoxicated on Imagination
Annabelle Dufourcq

Ruin Ecology: An Exercise in Environmental Imagination
Marco Malvestio

A full series listing is available at: www.cambridge.org/EIEH

Printed by Integrated Books International,
United States of America